W9-CER-077

Origins of the West Reader

Edited by Gregory Murry

Invino Academic Publishing
Hanover, PA

© Invino Academic Publishing, 2019
All Rights Reserved

Cover Image Courtesy of Dreamstime

Table of Contents

The Classical Imagination

By Sean Lewis

Imagine for a moment that you were born into and lived in a very different world than that of 21st-century America. You were born in the same general area as your great-grandparents, and you take for granted that your great-grandchildren will be born in the same place. From a very young age, you knew exactly what was expected of you, and how your life would play out, almost certainly doing the same work as your parents and extended family, which you began assisting in while you were still young. Your knowledge is relatively narrow: you are only aware of the customs, practices, and habits of thought prevalent in your homeland, and perhaps those that border you. These customs, practices, and habits of thought were passed down from your ancestors: you consider them to be of utmost authority, and certainly true. While your traditional knowledge is relatively narrow, it is quite deep: you likely know the history and legend of just about every part of your home, and you are intimately aware of the rhythms of nature: the cycle of the seasons and the movements of the heavens. These rhythms are the foundations for how you understand time. While you grow and mature, you see your life as part of a recurring natural cycle. It is almost impossible for you to imagine yourself as an individual: you are essentially a part of your community. When you approach the end of your life, having handed on this way of being to your children and grand-children, you will expect some sort of existence after death. It probably will simply be a shadow of this current existence, but you know from your ancestral habits of thought that gods and spirits permeate all of nature, and your own spirit will play a role in that natural order. You trust that your spirit will watch over your descendants for eternity, and that your great-grandchildren will pray to your spirit for protection and guidance.

The mode of human existence outlined above is likely quite different from the life you have lived, yet it was the way that the vast majority of the humans who have existed lived their lives. The culture of the Modern West, which has so formed the way we imagine the world, is a relatively new invention, one that will be explored in more depth in WCIV 201: Western Imagination. Origins of the West will deal with what, for lack of a better term, might be called the classical imagination: how humans in the pre-modern world imagined reality. The authority of the tradition in which a person lived was the primary source of knowledge. Individual liberty, the freedom to choose to be whatever you wanted, was unusual, and radically limited by the demands of community. The notion of progress did not exist: time moved as a cycle, and the order of the world was considered eternal.

The reason we begin our Culture and Civilization sequence with the classical imagination is twofold. On the one hand, in order to understand how radically unusual our own time and culture are, we need to consider the cultures of the past, cultures that represent what was "normal" for human beings for millennia, studying them through their historical, artistic, and literary products. On the other hand, the classical imagination is not as distant from us as we may think. The cultures and religions that we will study this semester are the originators of many of our own traditions. If we want to "know ourselves", or as our undergraduate mission statement puts it "understand the cultural forces operating on us," we need to under-stand how the culture which we inhabit came to be.

As we shall see, a vital part of the story of the origins of the West is the development of the ability to formulate critical opinions, and, ultimately, have the courage to engage in *self*-criticism. This course will carry on that tradition by challenging you to understand what culture means, to gain familiarity with the classical cultural traditions that shape the world in which we live, and to ask questions about how and when your beliefs and values might require you to be 'counter-cultural.'

If we want to form ourselves in ethical leadership in any meaningful way, we need to cultivate habits of reflection and self-criticism. We will do so in this course by engaging some of the great texts that have inspired ethical leaders for generations, from the classical agrarian world described in the opening paragraph to the innovators of the 21st century. It is quite a rich tradition of discourse, disagreement, and pursuit of truth, and it is a tradition that you will now begin to engage with in a self-conscious manner.

The Polytheistic Imagination

It is important to note that the texts we will be studying from ancient Greece, Rome, and Africa arise in the context of a polytheistic imagination, with divinity imagined as a plurality of entities. The major pantheons included gods who were patrons of every part of human life: fatherhood, motherhood, war, arts, fertility, language, healing, and death. Even though a given culture would reach a general consensus on the nature of the major pantheon, religious life was dominated by local divinities: families, towns, and parts of nature were watched over by specific gods or spirits.

Consider how you would view the world differently if you saw the natural world populated by an untold myriad of divine entities, entities who often behaved exactly like human beings, both for good and for ill. If you recognized a plurality of gods, the existence of foreign gods would not be unusual, and the polytheistic imagination, from our perspective, was simultaneously highly tolerant and highly bigoted. A foreigner's mother-goddess could simply be a different name for the mother-goddess you worshipped: various kinds of polytheisms could peacefully coexist. At the same time, gods played favorites, and you wanted to stay on your own gods' good sides: you were always on the side of your own gods, rather than the gods of other people. Religious identity was thus linked to civic and local identity, a habit of thinking and behavior handed down from ancestral times.

Chapter One

Democracy and the Athenian Golden Age

By Teresa Rupp

Many of the origins of our own culture come from the Greeks, an ethno-linguistic group who moved into the southern tip of the Balkan Peninsula around 2,000 BC. Greeks usually identified with a city-state (*polis*), a political entity that included a city and its surrounding area. By the middle of the classical period, the two most powerful ones were Sparta, a militaristic city-state that lay on the southern Peloponnese, and Athens, which lay on the Attic peninsula.

During the classical era in Greece, most *poleis* (city-states) were oligarchies, from the Greek for "rule by the few." The "few" in this case was defined as "those with money." Typically, the citizen body was divided into several classes based on their level of wealth, which determined the form of their military service. (Citizens served in the army at their own expense; they were not paid, and they had to furnish all their own equipment). So the wealthiest served in the cavalry (horses are expensive); the next-wealthiest served in the infantry (as hoplites in the phalanx); the next-wealthiest served as auxiliary, light-armed troops, and the poorest did not serve at all (because they couldn't afford to). A citizen's level of military service then determined his level of political service. Cavalrymen were eligible for all offices; an infantryman might be eligible for minor offices or an advisory body, and the lowest classes were ineligible to participate at all.

The Growth of Athenian Democracy

Until 508, Athens was an oligarchy as well. In that year, however, an Athenian aristocrat named Cleisthenes created democracy, or rule (*kratia*) by the people (*demos*, which refers specifically to the citizen body). As Pericles put it in 431 BC:

> Our laws give equal rights to all in private disputes, but public preferment depends on individual distinction and is determined largely by merit rather than rotation: and poverty is no barrier to office, if a man despite his humble condition has the ability to do some good to the city.

In other words, Athens did the opposite of what everybody else did. *All* male citizens, regardless of wealth, could participate actively in Athenian government. This is partly because of the importance of the navy in Athens. Each trireme (a warship powered by three banks of oars) had a crew of 200, and the fleet was made up of 300 triremes. That's a lot of rowers. Even poor citizens could serve as rowers because it didn't cost them anything. Unlike hoplites, who had to pay for spear, shield, and body armor, all a rower had to do was show up (and provide his own seat cushion). So in Athens, even the lowest class of citizens had an active military role.

Because the assumption was that military service entitled you to a political role, as Athens increased its reliance on its navy during the fifth century the rowers demanded (and got) a more active part in the government of the polis. This is known as "trireme democracy."

The Mechanics of Athenian Democracy

A citizen in the Athens of Pericles' day had a variety of opportunities for political activity. All male citizens, by definition, were members of the *ekklesia*, or assembly, which was the sovereign body of the state. The *ekklesia* made the laws and set both foreign and domestic policy. Though it is estimated that around 40,000 men were eligible to serve, scholars believe that only around 6,000 at a time actually took the opportunity.

Six thousand is a big number, and the Athenians recognized that carrying out the day-to-day business of the state with such a large group of people was impractical. So the Council of 500, or *Boule*, was chosen by lot each year to serve as an advisory body to the *ekklesia*. The *Boule* drew up the agenda for the *ekklesia* and supervised the conduct of public officials. Even 500 is an unwieldy group of people, so the Athenians divided the year into 10 equal segments, called *prytanies*, and 50 members of the *Boule* at a time functioned as an executive committee (*prytany* refers both to the division of time and to the committee itself). Each day, the current *prytany* chose (again by lot) a chairman, who presided over any meetings of the *prytany*, the whole *boule*, or the *ekklesia* held on that day.

Another way a citizen could participate in Athenian democracy was by serving on a jury. There was no public prosecutor (like our District Attorneys); instead, all cases were initiated by private citizens.[1] Such cases were then heard by courts made up of citizen-juries. Each year a panel of 6,000 jurors was chosen by lot; juries for

---

[1] This lack of lawyers in classical Athens promoted the practice of the rhetorical arts; an individual on trial would have to represent himself before the court and could not rely on the eloquence of another. Many rhetorical manuals were written in Athens, often focusing on how people could manipulate the emotions of the judge or jury. Both Plato and Aristotle took issue with these rhetorical manuals and their writers: the sophists. Plato's dialogues (*Gorgias, Sophist,* and *Phaedrus)* make the case that rhetoric is immoral and that dialectic alone should be the model for arguments. Aristotle wrote his own book on rhetoric (*The Rhetoric*), which responded to the sophists by including appeals to reason (*logos*) and character (*ethos*) along with appeals to emotion (*pathos*), and by considering more carefully different kinds of speeches and audiences. Sean Lewis footnote.

individual cases were then selected from that pool. Individual juries had hundreds of jurors (not just 12, like we do); 501 jurors tried Socrates, for example. Jurors were paid by the day for their service, so anyone could serve.

Along with the large democratic bodies, Athens had some magistrates—public officials whose job was to carry out the policies approved by the assembly. The most important of these were the *archons*, nine men chosen every year by lot; there were also some minor officials who had duties like supervising weights and measures in the *agora* (marketplace).

In the fifth century, all officials, members of councils, jurors, etc. were chosen by lot. This was a characteristic feature of democracy— it ensured that every citizen had an equal chance. No one could gain any advantage from his wealth, family name, or personal charm. However, there was one exception to this rule: the office of *strategos*, or military commander, the only elective office that remained under the democracy. Each year the *ekklesia* elected a board of ten *strategoi*, or generals, who led the army and navy. The Athenians reasoned that these officials actually needed to know what they were doing. As the only men chosen for their talents, the *strategoi* tended to be influential in more than military matters; their opinion carried a lot of weight because they were respected. This is the position that Pericles held: he was elected *strategos* many times in the mid-fifth century, and every year from 443 BC until his death in 429.[2]

Most democratic functions, as we have seen, were designed to be performed by the citizen body at large, regardless of wealth. But a few special functions were reserved for the rich. These were the liturgies (literally, "public works"). The liturgy was a way of financing expensive public activities without levying taxes; the rich paid for them directly as part of their civic duty. For example, rich citizens (known as *trierarchs*) built and equipped the triremes in the navy. Another type of liturgy was to sponsor a religious festival, especially

---

[2] Sophocles, author of *Antigone*, served as *strategos*, and legend has it that he was elected because of the quality of *Antigone*.

the festival of Dionysus where the tragedies were performed. A rich citizen known as a *choregos* financed the production of the plays.

Ostracism

A final feature of Athenian democracy was ostracism. To guard against any one person becoming too powerful (and possibly becoming a tyrant), the citizen body could vote someone into exile. Each year the assembly voted on whether or not to hold an ostracism. If the vote was yes, then later in the year a vote would be taken to decide who it would be. Citizens would gather in the *agora* (marketplace) and write the name of the person they wished to be exiled on a potsherd (a broken piece of pottery). The Greek word for potsherd is *ostrakon*, which is the origin of the word ostracism. The "winner" was exiled for ten years. Thousands of *ostraka* with names scratched on them have been found by archaeologist.

The First Persian War, 490 BC

At the beginning of the fifth century BC, the Greek cities on the Ionian coast revolted against Persian rule, aided by Athens. At first, these revolts were successful, but eventually the Persian Empire crushed them. Then the Persians turned their attention to punishing the Athenians.

In 490 BC, the Persian Emperor Darius sent a small fleet across the Aegean Sea to punish Athens, landing at Marathon on the coast of Attica. The Athenian army won the Battle of Marathon with expert use of the hoplite phalanx.

The Persians left and stayed away for the next 10 years because of internal difficulties in the Persian Empire.

The Second Persian War, 480-79

In 480 BC, the new Persian Emperor Xerxes sent a much larger expedition under his personal command across the Hellespont into Greece. The Greek alliance (Hellenic League), led by the Spartan

King Leonidas, met the Persian force at a narrow pass at Thermopylae in northern Greece.

At the Battle of Thermopylae, the Greeks held off the Persians until they were betrayed and surrounded. Leonidas sent the whole Greek army away except for 300 Spartans. They fought to the last man to delay the Persian advance.

At the Battle of Salamis, Themistocles, an Athenian *strategos*, convinced the Athenians to evacuate Athens. Women and children went to the mainland, and men took the fleet of triremes to the island of Salamis. The outnumbered Athenian fleet defeated the Persian fleet at the Battle of Salamis because of the triremes' superior speed and maneuverability. Most of the surviving Persians returned to Persia; a small remnant was defeated by the allied army of Athens and Sparta at the Battle of Plataea in 479 BC.

Athens then formed the Delian League, an alliance of Greek city-states designed to defend against future Persian invasion. The Delian League took its name from the original meeting place, the island of Delos. Athens, however, gradually began to exercise more control over the smaller states, and in 454 BC, Pericles moved the treasury to Athens. By the outbreak of the Peloponnesian War, the Delian League had come to look more like an Athenian empire than a partnership of equal city-state.

The Acropolis Project

In 447, Pericles launched an audacious rebuilding program of the Acropolis, the large hill in the middle of Athens that housed its most important temples. Pericles had in mind the idea that he'd build a lasting monument to Athenian greatness. The program included a number of temples and other public buildings, the grandest of which was the Parthenon, built to house a statue of Athen's patron deity: Athena, goddess of wisdom, war, and olives.[3]

Many of the sculptures on the exterior of the Parthenon express the theme of order overcoming chaos, a theme that would have had particular resonance to Athenians proud of their role in beating back the Persian Empire. The Parthenon is one of the great masterpieces of Western Civilization, copied by almost every subsequent western society. In its outlines, the Parthenon looks like a great number of other Greek temples; its base forms a rectangular box, and the exterior faces utilize a post and lintel structure, with simple Doric columns running along all sides. Nevertheless, the Parthenon was an innovative work of architecture. On the one hand, its unusually numerous columns and its position atop the Acropolis make it a fearsome expression of monumental building.[4] On the other hand, its proportions are harmonic and its lines graceful, designed to create the illusion of perfect straightness. The columns bulge slightly in the middle, so as to give the almost subconscious impression that they are human-like figures, drawing breath to lift the pediment. Because of this, the Parthenon needed to be constructed piece by piece and block by block, with each individual piece fitting into only one part of the temple. Despite that, the Athenians finished the work in a mere nine years (447-438 BC).[5]

To finish such a large building project in such a short amount of time required enormous sums of money. Pericles only persuaded the Athenian assembly to agree to the cost by shaming them into it, arguing that if they refused, he would fund the project himself and put his own name on it. However, much of the funding came from

---

[3] Sarah Pomeroy, Stanley Burstein, Walter Donlan, and Jennifer Tolbert Roberts, *Ancient Greece: A Political, Social, and Cultural History* (New York: Oxford University Press, 1999), 274-281.

[4] Thomas Martin, *Ancient Greece* (New Haven: Yale University Press, 2013), 120-121.

[5] *Secrets of the Parthenon*, directed by Michael Beckham and Gary Glassman (Nova, 2008).

Athen's theoretical allies in the Delian League, whose contributions to the mutual defense league were diverted to the building project instead.[6] Ironically then, this temple to Athenian democracy could only be funded by Athenian empire.

The Peloponnesian War: The First Phase, 431-421 BC

After a series of incidents involving disputes between the allies of both sides, war broke out in 431 BC between the Spartan alliance and the Athenian alliance (the Delian League).

Under the leadership of Pericles, Attica was evacuated and the population took refuge within the walls of Athens, both the city walls and the "Long Walls" that extended from the city to the port of Piraeus. Food imports were protected because of the Athenian navy's control of the Aegean Sea.

Pericles intended to fight a war of attrition—refusing to engage the Spartan hoplite army in a battle the Spartans were sure to win, while harassing the Peloponnesian coast with naval raids. But after Pericles' death in the plague, the unpopular policy was abandoned.

After several years of indecisive fighting, the Athenian *strategos* Nicias negotiated a truce meant to last for 50 years. Outside of a few minor skirmishes (such as the invasion of Melos in 416), this period of "cold war" lasted for only seven years.

The Final Phase, 414-404 BC

In 414 BC, Alcibiades (a handsome Athenian aristocrat and admirer of Socrates) convinced the Athenian assembly that the way to break the stalemate and defeat Sparta outright was to increase Athenian strength by conquering Sicily, then a populous and prosperous island. Athens launched a major expedition to Sicily in 414. The fleet was soundly defeated in a battle in the harbor of Syracuse. Thucydides' account of the Sicilian Expedition reads like

---

[6] Plutarch, *Plutarch's Lives* vol. 1 (New York: Modern Library, 2001), 214.

a retelling of the Second Persian War, with the Athenians in the role of the imperialistic Persians and Syracuse playing the part of the liberty-loving Athenians.

Accused of taking part in a religious scandal on the eve of the fleet's departure for Sicily, Alcibiades fled to Sparta, where he brokered a deal with the Persians to supply Sparta with funds to build a navy.

After several years of trying, the Spartan navy finally defeated the Athenian navy at the Battle of Aegospotami in 404. Following the destruction of their fleet, Athens surrendered.

In the wake of their defeat, the Athenians looked for a scapegoat. They found one in the philosopher and social critic Socrates, who among other things had been a friend and teacher to the disgraced and traitorous Alcibiades. In 399 BC, the Athenians tried Socrates and found him guilty of impiety and corrupting the youth of Athens. For this crime, he was sentenced to death

Chapter Two

Greek Theater

By Sean Lewis

Greek tragedy is a foundational art in the Western imagination; the works of Aeschylus, Sophocles, and Euripides have inspired readers and audiences in almost every period of Western civilization. We continue to think and talk about great political and historical figures as though they are "tragic heroes": leaders as different as Napoleon and Lincoln have been spoken of in tragic terms.

There must have been numerous playwrights in ancient Greece, but only thirty-one tragedies have survived out of the thousands that were written. Aeschylus (c. 523-456), Sophocles (c. 496-406), and Euripides (c. 480-406) are the three authors whose works display the origins of our ideas of tragedy. This course is giving you a mere taste of the grandeur of Greek tragedy, and if it catches your interests, you should engage in more in-depth studies of theatre history. What this brief introduction seeks to give you is some context and vocabulary to understand and analyze Sophocles' *Antigone*, allowing you to approach this great tragedy on its own terms.[7]

---

[7] Information for this chapter comes primarily from Oscar G. Brockett and Franklin J. Hildy, *History of the Theatre* (New York: Pearson, 2007), A.M Nagler, *A Source Book in Theatrical History* (New York: Dover, 1959), and Aristotle, *Poetics*, trans. Ingram Bywater (New York: Modern

The Experience of Greek Theater

What would it have felt like to be an Athenian attending the opening of Sophocles' *Antigone*? Let's first talk about the setting. Plays in ancient Greece were performed in conjunction with religious festivals honoring Dionysus, god of fertility, wine, and partying whose cult spread throughout Greece from its origins in the Middle East; the frenzied nature of Dionysian worship provides the basis for our very word "tragedy", which literally means "goat song." The major Dionysian festivals celebrated in Athens were the Rural Dionysia, the Lenaia, the Anthesteria, and the City Dionysia. This last celebration is most significant for our purposes, since it was at this early springtime festival that dramatic competitions occurred in the city of Athens. Over the course of about a week, Athens would be the site of religious rites honoring Dionysius, followed by dramas. According to Aristotle's *Poetics*, dramas grew out of improvised song competitions (1449a), but by the fifth century these plays had taken on a developed, complex form.[8] Playwrights wishing to enter the competition had to produce a trilogy of tragedies, whose plots were drawn almost exclusively from mythology. In addition to the trilogy, playwrights provided a fourth drama, the satyr play, a burlesque, bawdy show that likely parodied the myths that were treated seriously in the tragedy (our word "satire" is ultimately derived from the satyr plays).[9] From the many dramatists who entered their plays

---

Library, 1984). I am very grateful for Dr. Kurt Blaugher's input in preparing this chapter.

[8] According to tradition, Thespis is honored as the first dramatist; he is credited with being the first actor to create dialogue between himself and the chorus. Other early dramatic figures are Choerilus (who supposedly first used costumes and masks), Pratinas (the inventor of the satyr play), and Phrynichus (the first playwright to use female characters).

[9] Satirical choruses were probably composed of men dressed as *actual* satyrs, the horned, goat-footed, continually drunken and sexually aroused creatures who followed Dionysius. 21st-century satirists seem downright tame in comparison.

18

for the competition, three were selected to compete for the prize, and over the course of several days, their plays would be performed for the public, originally either in the marketplace (the *agora*) or in a park dedicated to Dionysius; by the late fifth century, a Theatre of Dionysus had been built by the Athenians for the specific purpose of housing these plays. After all the plays were performed, judges chosen by lot would cast their votes, and the winning playwright received a prize and often a monument.

All of this background should indicate that if you were an Athenian seeing the first production of *Antigone*, you would not have been seeing a brand new story; the myth of the house of Laius was well-known, and the play would have been part of a tragic trilogy. In fact, of the few Greek tragedies that have survived, two of them demonstrate that Sophocles treated the house of Laius more than once: *Oedipus Rex* and *Oedipus at Colonus* tell the tragic story of King Oedipus of Thebes, who unwittingly killed his father Laius, married his own mother (Jocasta), and was so distraught over this horrible situation that he blinded himself and sent himself into exile.[10] The story of Antigone and her struggle to bury her brother Polyneices in defiance of her uncle, King Creon, would have been encountered with Oedipus in mind: Oedipus defying the blind prophet Tiresias, realizing the awful truth of his past, and suffering through exile with his daughters Antigone and Ismene. The action of *Antigone*, then, is the culmination of a cycle of traditional myths about the doomed house of Thebes; the pleasure and wonder for the original audience lay not in seeing a new story performed before them, but rather from experiencing the way in which Sophocles told it, acted before their eyes during a time of celebration.

---

[10] Freud would later use the Oedipus myth to create his famous "Oedipus complex," the theory that all boys unconsciously want to kill their fathers and have sex with their mothers. While Freud's theories have been subsequently discredited by psychologists, they remain common cultural myths to this day.

The Setting of Greek Theater

As stated above, these communal dramas would have been performed outdoors, eventually in an amphitheater, which consisted of stadium seating (they were built into sides of hills and mountains, plentiful landmarks in rocky Greece), focused on a circular performance space (the orchestra), behind which was a structure that served as both a background and a stage for the action (the *skene*). The acoustics in these theaters are works of genius; in the Theater at Epidaurus, for example, a speaker standing in the orchestra, projecting in even a moderate voice, can be heard throughout the over 10,000 seats in the theater even to this day! Microphones were unnecessary for ancient Greek actors, and surviving documents recount their beautiful vocal prowess. Other pieces of engineering would have included painted panels that would have been used for scenery (*pinakes*, simple panels, and *periaktoi*, panels that could turn to change scenes) and cranes (*machinai*) used to make divine characters ascend or descend (the origin of our phrase *deus ex machina*—the god from the machine).[11]

The Roles of Greek Drama

One way of understanding the actors in Greek drama is to divide them into distinct categories: the protagonist, the deuteragonist, the tritagonist, the *koryphaios* (chorus leader), and the chorus.[12] Of these,

---

[11] In drama, a "deus ex machina" is often used to refer to a not terribly realistic or satisfying resolution to the problem in a plot. Rather than resolving itself naturally, some kind of unrealistic good fortune comes in from the outside and fixes all the problems. For an example of a *deus ex machina*, consider the climax of *Harry Potter and the Chamber of Secrets*; the magical phoenix happens to fly down at exactly the right time to give Harry the weapon and medicine necessary to kill the basilisk and heal his wound. How terribly convenient!

[12] Aeschylus is credited with inventing the deuteragonist, Sophocles with the tritagonist.

only the first four were single actors; the chorus was a collection of actors who sang and danced the choral sections. The protagonist (a term still used today) played the central character, the deuteragonist the secondary main characters, generally in conflict with the protagonist,[13] and the tritagonist the minor parts; notice that actors in Greek drama were thought of in terms of struggle or conflict: *agon* is Greek for contest or struggle, and the primary two actors are, literally, the first contender and the second contender.

Actors wore large masks to depict their characters; the masks of Greek drama allowed a few actors to depict multiple characters (although the protagonist probably stayed in the same role for the entire drama).[14] The fact that there were only three main actors accounts for an oddity that you might notice: there are never more than three characters on stage at a single time in Sophocles' tragedies. The chorus, however, would interact with the dialogue and action of the characters, commenting on the action. You will also notice sections of *Antigone* that consist entirely of the chorus singing about what you have just witnessed occur on stage. For these purposes, the chorus sometimes splits, with a choral leader (*koryphaios*) performing some sections and the entire chorus responding; these choral sections are structured around *strophes* and *antistrophes* (turns and counter-turns), in which the chorus debates or mulls over vital questions, problems, or truths: pay special attention to the famous first Ode on Man (c. 280) that the chorus performs at a vital point in the play's action: how is their song commenting on characters or events at that point in the drama? These debates bring to mind unresolved (or unresolvable?) tensions in Greek culture and human nature itself.

---

[13] Critics to this day argue about whether Antigone or Creon is the protagonist of *Antigone*. Which one makes more sense to you? How does the drama change if we understand Creon to be the protagonist? Much thanks to Dr. Blaugher for pointing out this controversy.

[14] As in Shakespeare's Elizabethan theater and the Noh drama of Japan, actors in ancient Greece were all male; masks helped with the depiction of female characters.

Greek Tragedy

Our critical terminology for tragedy originates with Aristotle's *Poetics*, and his categories may be of great help to you as you come to grips with *Antigone*. In the first place, Aristotle identifies six constituent parts of drama: plot (*mythos*), character (*ethos*), thought (*dianoia*), diction (*lexis*), song (*melopoiia*), and spectacle (*opsis*), and he treats them in what he finds to be a descending order of importance. For Aristotle, plot is far more important than character, since without conflict and action there is no drama; he went so far as to say, "plot is the soul of tragedy" (*psyche ho mythos tes tragoidias*, 1450a). While you can use these categories productively to analyze the tragedy, do consider the importance of the "lesser" elements of drama: music and spectacle (which would include costumes, blocking, and choreography). Even if these are less "essential" than the plot and characters, are they then utterly *un*necessary? Reading a drama is far different from seeing one performed, and do not think that Aristotle is selling short the wonder of live theater.

Aristotle also gave us a vocabulary to understand tragic characters. According to Aristotle, tragic figures often exhibit *hubris*, violent action, arising from the pride of strength or passion[15] that leads to their ruin or the ruin of loved ones. Which characters in *Antigone* seem to display *hubris*, and how does this *hubris* relate to the tragic action of the play? Tragic characters often commit a *hamartia*, a fatal error of judgment (literally "missing the mark"), which they may make, as in the case of Oedipus, completely unwittingly.[16] This *hamartia* leads to their downfall: which characters in *Antigone* commit *hamartiai*, and what are the consequences of these errors of judgment? Finally, Aristotle talks about plots having *desis* (binding) and *lysis* (loosing)—the actions of the characters lead to successive complications, binding them in different ways and leading up to a

---

[15] Liddell and Scott's Greek-English Lexicon (Oxford: Clarendon Press, 1966), 723, "ΎΒΡΙΣ".

[16] Looking ahead to the Bible, *hamartia* is the word used in the Septuagint and the New Testament to refer to sin.

climactic moment at which the difficulties begin to loosen, leading to a resolution of the central problem of the plot. The *desis* and *lysis* can be thought of in terms of *peripeteia* (reversal) and *anagnorisis* (revelation): at a certain point, the protagonist suffers a turn in fate (*peripeteia*) that is often accompanied or followed by a revelation about the state of affairs previously unknown to the character (*anagnorisis*). What points in the text of *Antigone* exhibit successive bindings or turns of fate? How are these tensions resolved? What revelations occur? All of these questions will help you think about *Antigone* using Greek dramatic terminology.

Another important Aristotelian term to learn in relation to Greek tragedy is *catharsis*; *catharsis* is the emotional "release" the audience receives through watching a drama. Think about the tears you shed in laughter or sorrow at watching spectacularly funny or sad movies: those are tears of catharsis in Aristotle's mind. Greek drama is supposed to lead to a purgation of emotion from the audience; in the case of tragedy, they are lead through fear and pity (*phobos* and *eleos*) in order to regain a psychological and spiritual balance. It should be no wonder, then, that theaters were often found at Greek healing temples: physicians could treat patients' bodies, while drama treated their souls and minds. Pay attention to your own response to the action of *Antigone*: how do pity and fear play roles? In what way is the end "satisfying" or not? Catharsis is an excellent way to talk about the effect of drama (or any of the arts) on the entire human person, physically, intellectually, and spiritually.

Finally, consider Aristotle's notion of *why* we enjoy watching drama; Aristotle claims that the origin of all poetry, including drama, comes from human nature itself (1448b). Human beings are essentially *mimetic*: we enjoy making and watching an imitation (*mimesis*) of nature. Aristotle points to the play of young children as evidence of this truth; you've probably encountered small children pretending to be animals, but almost certainly not small animals pretending to be children. The mimetic nature of human beings means that we can choose what to imitate, and which imitations we want to experience; later literary critics will tie *mimesis* with ethics:

we form our character (*ethos*) by imitating the characters encountered in literary and historical works.[17] More essentially, however, the imitations we watch shape who we are and how we imagine the world; myths, stories, and narratives, both fictional and non-fictional, are an essential way we human beings think about ourselves and our world. Pay attention to what *Antigone* is "saying" about human life through the way it imitates it, and what truths this imitation may reveal.

---

[17] Wayne O. Booth is a recent supporter of this school of literary criticism; see *The Company We Keep: An Ethics of Fiction* (Berkeley and Los Angeles: University of California Press, 1988). One of the more eloquent supporters of this way of understanding literature, however, is Sir Philips Sydney, whose 1595 *Defense of Poesy* makes the claim that reading good poetry helps make you a good person.

Chapter Three

Rome: From Republic To Empire

By Teresa Rupp and Gregory Murry

Rome was founded as a small city-state, sitting atop seven hills near the Tiber River in 753 BC. Legend has it that the city was established as a sanctuary for shepherds, criminals and runaway slaves. For the first two hundred or so years, Rome was ruled by kings, who expanded the rule (*imperium*) of the Romans over the surrounding peoples. At the end of the sixth century, under the leadership of Lucius Junius Brutus, the Romans expelled the last king, Tarquin the Proud, and established a republic. The Roman Republic was a mixed regime type; the constitution provided for democratic elements (the assemblies of the people), oligarchical elements (the senate), and monarchical elements (two consuls, who were elected to serve one-year terms). Republican Rome continued to expand its empire in the following centuries. By 300 BC, the Romans controlled most of the Italian peninsula. By the end of the Emperor Augustus' reign in 14 AD, the Roman Empire stretched from the Iberian Peninsula in the west to modern-day Turkey in the east and from the English Channel in the north to the Red Sea in the south.

The Conquest of Italy

Roman imperialism was defensive—based on their experience, they regarded every neighbor as a potential enemy. Once they had neutralized that neighbor/enemy, either by means of conquest or alliance, they acquired new neighbors. The result was the expansion of Roman power, first over the Italian peninsula, then, eventually, over the Mediterranean.

As the Romans expanded from their original settlement on the Tiber River northwards and southwards, they developed a descending system of privileges, based on distance from Rome. Inhabitants of territories closest to the city were granted full Roman citizenship. Those next closest, e.g. in the region of Latium, were granted Latin Rights (the rights of the people of Latium), which was equivalent to Roman citizenship except for the right to vote and hold office. Anyone with Latin rights who moved to the city moved up to full Roman citizenship. Those farthest away were granted Italian Rights, which was an alliance—they agreed to "have the same friends and enemies" as Rome, and to provide soldiers for the Roman army (as did the citizens and the Latins).

The Punic Wars

Once Italy was in Roman hands, the next "neighbor" was Sicily, at the time a part of the empire of Carthage. The series of wars the Romans fought against the Carthaginians are called the Punic Wars from the Latin word for Phoenician; Carthage was originally a colony of the Phoenicians.

The First Punic War (264-241 BC) was fought for control of Sicily. It was long and difficult, but the Romans eventually won (this is an all-purpose sentence for Roman history). After their victory, the Romans had to decide what to do with Sicily. Instead of giving it Italian rights, for security reasons the Romans instead made it a province—the first province of the Roman Empire. Provinces were governed directly by Rome (instead of being self-governing, like the allies) and were required to pay taxes (instead of providing soldiers, like the allies).

The Second Punic War (218-202 BC) was fought for control of the entire western Mediterranean. It was long and difficult, but the Romans eventually won. This was the conflict during which Hannibal invaded Italy by crossing the Alps with his army and his war elephants. He stayed in Italy for 15 years, devastating the Italian countryside. He was unable, however, either to attack the city of Rome itself or to convince the allies to betray Rome. The war finally ended when Publius Cornelius Scipio Africanus[18] took the war to North Africa. Hannibal was recalled to defend the homeland; Scipio defeated him at the battle of Zama in 202 BC. After the Roman victory, the former territories of the Carthaginian Empire were made into Roman provinces.

The Third Punic War (149-146 BC) was almost an afterthought. All that was left of the Carthaginian Empire was the city of Carthage. Marcus Cato was convinced that Carthage was a threat—as long as Carthage survived, Rome would not be safe. Cato famously concluded all his speeches in the senate, on whatever topic they happened to be on, with the phrase, "In conclusion, Carthage must be destroyed." Eventually, he convinced the senate to besiege the city, which surrendered in 146 BC after a three-year siege. The city was destroyed and the land sowed with salt, to prevent its ever being rebuilt. The territory surrounding Carthage was made into the province of Africa.

---

[18] Romans usually had three names: the praenomen, the nomen, and the cognomen. The praenomen (the first name) was a personal name, chosen by the parents at birth (Publius). The nomen (middle name) was the family name, indicating the individual's gens or tribe (Cornelius from the gens Cornelia). The cognomen (third name) was like a nickname: Romans could have many of these. Some were hereditary (Scipio); some were given for accomplishments (Africanus or the African, since he subdued Carthage). Keep these naming conventions in mind as we encounter other Romans; Quintus Horatius Flaccus is Horace to us; Publius Vergilius Maro is Virgil. Sean Lewis footnote.

The Macedonian Wars

In the east, the Romans took a different approach. They fought the Macedonian Wars (200-146 BC) for control of the eastern Mediterranean. The Hellenistic kingdom of Macedon had aided Hannibal in the Second Punic War; after the victory over Hannibal, it needed to be punished. These wars were long and difficult, but the Romans eventually won. After each victory, however, the Romans tried to avoid making the defeated territories into provinces, which are, after all, a lot of trouble to run. Instead, they tried making them into client-states—allies that would "have the same friends and enemies," run themselves, give the Romans no trouble, and act as a buffer between the Romans and hostile territories farther away. But the Greeks didn't know how to be good clients. They thought being independent of the Romans meant they were free—free to fight among themselves, as they always had. The Romans would have to keep coming back and settling things between them. Eventually the Romans gave up and made their eastern territories into provinces as well.

Governors: The Proconsuls

The acquisition of this empire caused the Romans a lot of problems. One problem was simply how to administer the provinces. The institutions that had grown up to run a city-state quickly proved inadequate for an overseas empire. Eventually the Romans developed the position of the proconsul to govern the provinces; proconsuls were former consuls who were assigned to govern a province after their term of office was up.

Tax Collection: The Publicans

Inhabitants of provinces (unlike Roman citizens) were required to pay taxes; taxes had to be collected somehow. Instead of developing a bureaucracy with salaried tax collectors, they came up with the solution of the publicans. Publicans were independent businessmen who were granted a contract to collect the taxes in a province. They were responsible to pay a set amount to Rome; whatever they collected above that amount they were free to keep as their profit. Publicans were greatly resented in the provinces because they were symbols of Roman rule and because they often grew wealthy from their share of the tax; for example, the Matthew of the Gospels was a publican.

Manpower: The *Latifundia*

As Rome's responsibilities increased, their manpower needs increased also. Soldiers in the Roman army were, like those in the Greek army, drawn from men who met a minimum property requirement, since they served at their own expense. But as Rome's responsibilities increased, fewer and fewer men were able to meet the property requirement. Hannibal's years in Italy had devastated Italian agriculture; furthermore, soldiers who were away on campaign for years at a time often lost their land. The result was that small family farms were gradually converted into *latifundiae*, large estates producing cash crops, mostly wine and olives, and worked by slaves (available because of the conquests). The displaced poor were forced to take refuge in the city, where they survived as clients of the wealthy and powerful. This situation would lead to years of civil war and eventually the end of the republic.

The Reforms of the Gracchi, 133 and 122 BC

Two brothers, Tiberius Sempronius Gracchus and Gaius Sempronius Gracchus, attempted to solve this manpower shortage. They proposed to distribute public land (not private property) to the poor, so more people would qualify for the army. They were opposed, not only by the wealthy who were illegally occupying this public land, but also by other senators, who realized that if the proposal went through, the Gracchi would gain potentially thousands of clients—the recipients of the land. During the ensuing unrest, both the Gracchi were assassinated (Tiberius in 133 BC and Gaius in 122 BC).

The Reforms of Marius

Gaius Marius took a different approach to the manpower shortage. As consul between 107 and 101 BC (note how the *mores maiorum*, the ancestral customs, were breaking down—traditionally consuls were not reelected) he faced a formidable enemy in the Numidians of North Africa and needed more soldiers than were available. Instead of giving them property, he eliminated the property requirement and began the practice of paying the soldiers. Rome's army therefore changed from citizen-soldiers to a professional army. Marius did this out of military necessity, but it had unintended consequences.

The Civil Wars

Between 100 and 44 BC, Rome suffered a series of civil wars between ambitious politicians (remember the story of Romulus and Remus!). They all followed essentially the same pattern. Ambitious Roman generals would use their armies to conquer Rome's latest enemies. The now-professional soldiers saw themselves not as serving the Republic but as clients of their generals—their source of livelihood, professional advancement, opportunities for plunder, and retirement benefits. The generals had to keep conquering in order to keep these benefits coming. When the Roman Senate didn't give them what they wanted, they used their soldiers as private armies to defeat their rivals. The result was the series of civil wars between Marius and Sulla, Pompey and Crassus, and finally Pompey and Caesar.

Julius Caesar

Finally, it became clear that the Republic could no longer survive. One-man rule was inevitable—but which man? Julius Caesar defeated his rival Pompey in 48 BC. He tried to cement his power by naming himself dictator, first for 10 years, then, in 44 BC for life. That turned out to be true—he was assassinated by a conspiracy of senators led by Brutus (a descendant of the Brutus who had expelled Tarquin) and Cassius in 44 BC.

The conspirators believed they were restoring the Republic. Instead, Caesar's assassination merely led to another series of civil wars, which ended in 31 BC with the victory of Julius Caesar's adopted son, Octavian (Augustus), who defeated his rivals Marc Antony and Cleopatra at the Battle of Actium.

The Rise of Augustus

Following the assassination of Julius Caesar, Octavian raised a private army and returned to Rome. There, he came into conflict with Marc Antony, who had incited the populace against the assassins during his funeral oration for Caesar, thereby chasing Brutus, Cassius and the other conspirators out of the city. Nevertheless, Antony refused to surrender Caesar's estate to Octavian or to support the young man's political ambitions. Thus, Octavian turned on Antony, securing influence in Rome by winning the favor of the foremost Roman senator, Marcus Tullius Cicero, whose treatise on friendship you should recall from the First-Year Symposium. Then Octavian put his army at the service of the senate and helped to defeat Antony in battle at Mutina in 43 BC. Following the victory, however, Octavian betrayed both the senate and Cicero (suggesting that Cicero was not very good at picking his friends) by forming a second triumvirate with Antony and another Roman general named Marcus Lepidus. The second triumvirate then joined forces to defeat Brutus and Cassius at the Battle of Philippi in 42 BC.

To his enemies, Octavian showed little mercy; after Philippi, he reportedly sent Brutus' severed head back to Rome to be laid at the feet of Julius Caesar's statue. Senators who opposed him, especially in his early years, could expect little better: Antony and Octavian executed hundreds of senators (including Cicero) and thousands of

Roman knights in order to eliminate political opponents and seize their wealth.

To avoid Caesar's fate, Octavian deputed the Praetorian Guard, elite soldiers who had served as the personal bodyguards of Roman generals in the field, to act as his own bodyguard in Rome. With his control of the army, he gradually eliminated all his rivals until he was the sole power left in the empire.[19] As Octavian gradually arrogated all the power in the republic to himself, he was very careful not to call himself a king. Rather, he adopted a number of other titles, such as *imperator* (one who exercises *imperium*), *princeps* (first man), son of the divine Julius Caesar, and Augustus (great one). He also carefully maintained the appearance that the republic still existed. He kept all the old structures of power in place, including the senate, whose consent he was careful to secure before enacting any important decisions. But his real power did not lay with the senate: it lay with his control of the army. Indeed, when he was only twenty years old, he led his legions to Rome and demanded that the senate make him a consul; when the senate hesitated, his military legate flashed the hilt of his sword and said, "This will make him consul if you will not."[20] After the defeat of Marc Antony at Actium in 31 BC, it was quite clear that Octavian was the sole power in Rome and that no important decisions could be made without his consent.

---

[19] Ibid., 54-112.

[20] Suetonius, *The Twelve Caesars*, trans. Robert Graves (London: Penguin, 1989), 67.

Chapter Four

The Roman Epic

By Sean Lewis

The Roots of Epic Poetry

In the early 21st century, the word "epic" has undergone an unfortunate shift in meaning. A particularly well-executed move on a skateboard or a rather shady road trip over spring break may be said to be "epic." It is the nature of language to change over time, but there is something particularly dissatisfying about this shift in meaning, since for most of Western Civilization, "epic" referred to a specific poetic mode, a poetic mode exalted by generations of readers (Aristotle included) as the highest form of literature. What the Bible is to Christians, epics were to the ancient Greeks and Romans. Epics told of gods and heroes, the histories of nations, and expressed deep truths about human nature. It is hard to overestimate the importance and influence of epic poetry to the Western world, and Augustan Rome witnessed the composition of one of the most influential epics of them all: Virgil's *Aeneid*.

Epic poetry began simply as hymns to the gods, part of the oral religious tradition of ancient Greece; the so-called *Homeric Hymns* are witnesses to these sorts of poems. At some point, songs began to be composed and sung about humans, not gods: the heroes of the classical age. As examples of oral poetry, these works had a highly improvisational quality: the singer could add or subtract sections at will, given the occasion and audience. The singer-poets of ancient Greece were able to achieve this improvisation through features like *heroic epithets*, stock phrases that were attached to a specific character ("ox-eyed Hera"; "circumspect Penelope"; "pious Aeneas"), *catalogues* or *lists* (Book II of the *Iliad* consists of a long list of ships from different Greek nations), and prefabricated episodes or dialogues. With a general sense of plot, and many of these features carried in memory, the singer-poet could weave great works of oral poetry.

Homer and Greek Epics

These heroic narratives developed through generations until, around the 8th century B.C., a poet conventionally known as Homer drew these oral traditions together to make the first two epics of the Western tradition: the *Iliad* and the *Odyssey*.[21] Both epics take as their matter characters and events surrounding the Trojan War (c. 1200 B.C.): the *Iliad* tells the story of the wrath of Achilles on the battlefield, while the *Odyssey* tells the story of Odysseus' journey home from the war. If you have not read these works, you should find a way to do so before graduating the Mount: these texts were quoted like Scripture by ancient Greeks, and formed the imaginations and characters of hundreds of generations. Plato and Aristotle quote

---

[21] Gallons of ink have been spilled regarding the question of whether Homer actually existed, and, if he existed, whether he wrote the two epics attributed to him. There are many assumptions in the former sentence that betray 19th-century prejudices about literary composition; contemporary scholarship gives the matter more nuance. It is clear that many of the features of *The Iliad* and *The Odyssey* are drawn from oral tradition that would have preceded Homer, yet these pre-existing materials were clearly put into intentional literary forms. Whether there was one poet or more than one poet, the act of writing these stories down, fixing their form in writing, was a great achievement, and the convention of calling the one who wrote these first epics "Homer" has yet to be superseded.

Homer consistently, and Alexander the Great took copies of Homer with him to inspire his deeds as he conquered the known world.

As literary achievements, it is important to note that these epics are *national* in character, giving a literary portrait of what it means to be Greek. Underscoring this pan-Hellenic vision is the fact that Homer's language is drawn from multiple Greek dialects: it is a kind of Greek intelligible across different *poleis*, but not the Greek spoken in any single *polis*. Besides creating a specifically *literary* version of the Greek language, Homer also created many of the conventions that would be followed by later writers of epics. Homer writes in dactylic hexameter, a meter that would be imitated by later Greek and Latin epic writers for its gravity. The action of the plot is often punctuated with long speeches delivered by single characters. Homer begins both epics with an *invocation*, asking the divine Muse to inspire him to be able to sing about such lofty events. He also starts the epic action *in media res* ("in the middle of the thing"), rather than beginning at the beginning of the plot; filmmakers to this day use this technique to great effect. Though the division of books in the epic is a creation of later editors of Homer, both of his epics have 24 books, corresponding to the 24 hours of a day, and suggesting that the totality of human life (or, at least, Greek life) could be found in its pages.

Virgil and the Aeneid

While many later Greek poets imitated Homer and wrote their own epics (the Cyclic Poets and the Alexandrian school were particularly noteworthy), the next major epic poet in the Western tradition came from Rome: Publius Vergilius Maro (70-19 BC.), commonly known to us as Virgil. Virgil lived in Augustan Rome, and, as we have seen, Roman culture was going through a process of redefinition as the Roman Republic transformed into an empire with Augustus at its head. Republican Roman poets had only infrequently ventured into epic territory; their favorite poetic form was didactic poetry, poetry aimed at teaching good *mores*. With the Augustan age, however, Roman poets began imitating the Greek epic in Latin, perhaps a natural move, since the epic not only praises great men and their deeds (Augustus?), but also seeks to understand the character of the specific nation that produced it. The *Iliad* and the *Odyssey* show us what it means to be Greek; what, particularly in the age of Augustus, did it mean to be Roman?

Virgil's answer was developed in the *Aeneid*, a masterpiece of epic poetry that combined the actions of both the *Iliad* and the *Odyssey* into the story of a single hero: pious Aeneas. Aeneas, a Trojan prince, has been given the duty of refounding Troy some-where else in the Mediterranean world; the first six books of the *Aeneid* are modelled on the wanderings of Odysseus in the *Odyssey*. Just as Odysseus is waylaid from his homecoming by the temptations of the nymph Calypso, so too is Aeneas distracted from his ultimate goal by Queen Dido of Carthage. Aeneas is faithful to the will of the gods, and ends up settling his Trojans in central Italy—they will intermarry with the local population and eventually become the Romans. Their Roman fate is made clear in Book VI of the *Aeneid*, when Aeneas journeys through the underworld to meet the ghost of his father Anchises, and Anchises points out the souls of his descendants (the great heroes of Roman history) while addressing Aeneas as a "Roman" and giving him his mission: "Roman, remember by your strength to rule / Earth's peoples—for your arts are to be these: / To pacify, to impose the rule of law, / To spare the conquered, battle down the proud."[22] This process of founding Rome will not, however, be a peaceful one, and the second six books of the *Aeneid* (VII-XII) recall the battlefields of the *Iliad* as Aeneas is forced to wage war with locals who oppose his mission. As Virgil began the *Aeneid in media res*, so he ends without a clear resolution: Aeneas pitilessly slaughters his rival Turnus on the battlefield; the last lines of the poem are: "[Aeneas] sank his blade in fury in Turnus' chest. / Then all the body slackened in death's chill, / And with a groan for

---

[22] Virgil, *The Aeneid*, trans. Robert Fiztgerald (New York: Vintage Classics, 1990), VI.1151-54.

that indignity / His spirit fled into the gloom below."[23] That's quite an odd way to end an epic, compared to Homer's models.

So, what is a Roman, according to Virgil's work? That, it turns out, is a tricky question. Virgil was patronized by Augustus, and many have read the *Aeneid* as simple political propaganda: Augustus' Rome is the divinely-willed culmination of a process that began at the end of the Trojan War, giving the Romans as noble and heroic a history as the Greeks (and, actually, a history *more* noble and heroic than the Greeks, whom they ended up conquering). Traditional Roman virtues are extolled: Aeneas displays *gravitas, magnitudo animi, constantia,* and *pietas,* and this last virtue is his defining characteristic: Aeneas is called "pious" more than any other heroic epithet. In fact, many early readers of the *Aeneid* read it as an allegory for the development of the soul: Aeneas is the soul, wandering through temptations (like Dido), but ultimately reaching maturity halfway through the epic (Aeneas' old nursemaid dies at the beginning of Book VII), and then applying his greatness of soul to fulfill his duty in the remainder of the work. St. Augustine was one such reader of the *Aeneid,* patterning his own life journey in the *Confessions* on Virgil's *Aeneid,* and Dante is led through Hell and Purgatory not by a Jewish prophet or a Christian saint, but by the pagan poet Virgil.

Virgil's epic supports such a reading, but there nevertheless remain deep ambiguities in the text. Virgil is unclear, for example, on the nature of his gods; while the pantheon are very real (and anthropomorphic) in Homer's world, it is often unclear whether Virgil's gods are real, or whether they are simply metaphors for natural and psychological phenomena: is there a real entity called Venus who forces Dido to fall in love with Aeneas, or is "Venus" simply a personification of sexual desire? The further the epic progresses, the less clear the answer becomes, which has important implications for how we read the plot: is Aeneas commanded to leave Dido by the gods, or does he simply choose to do so, the gods being

---

[23] Ibid., XII.1295-98.

personifications of his own mind and will? In the moral reading of the *Aeneid*, Dido is nothing but an unhappy distraction (*infelix*, "unhappy," is her most common epithet); if the gods do not really exist, her status needs to be reevaluated. Another example of ambiguity is the Roman character. Yes, Aeneas is the example of a perfect Roman, yet he becomes an oddly impersonal hero: he sacrifices all of his private goods for the common good, which is a very Roman ideal. What Virgil leaves, though, is a character who becomes increasingly flat: Aeneas at the beginning of the epic is much more vibrant and developed than the Aeneas who ends the epic. Are Roman virtues ultimately fulfilling? Finally, there is the matter of the ending of the epic: Rome has been given the divine charge to bring law and peace to the world, but the epic ends in the middle of a battle. There is no clean resolution to the plot of the *Aeneid*, and it seems as though the only way that Romans bring law and peace is through constant, brutal war. In terms of literary history and influence, reading the *Aeneid* as a straightforward example of Roman virtue was clearly the preferred mode of interpretation, but Virgil's own literary achievement rests on deep ambiguity over the nature of the Roman character.

Chapter Five

The Empire of Gana and Gassire's Lute

By Gregory Murry and Sean Lewis

The opening chapter of this textbook indicated that there were certain broad habits of thought and action common across the classical imagination, regardless of geographical area or specific culture. Because of their influence on subsequent culture and civilization, we have focused on texts that arose in Classical Greece and Rome. Greece and Rome are not, however, the only classical civilizations, and a study of the classical cultures of Asia and Africa displays many parallels.

We are now going to turn to an example of the classical imagination from Africa, more specifically from the semi-arid grasslands of West Africa known as the Sahel, which is bordered by the Sahara to the north and the wetter savanna to the south. These are territories that are roughly encompassed by portions of the modern-day nation-states of Mali, Mauritania, Senegal, and Burkina Faso. By 400 AD, peoples in the Sahel had begun to construct sophisticated, urban civilizations, with relatively large towns and sedentary agricultural practices. Starting around 700 AD, various peoples living in the western Sahel had begun to develop the first of three successive empires: the Ganian, The Malian, and the Songhay.

Ganian Society

The earliest of the great Sahelian kingdoms was the Empire of Gana, which flourished from roughly 800 AD to 1200 AD. The Empire of Gana is not to be confused with the modern nation-state of Ghana. The founders of modern Ghana chose the name to honor the medieval empire, but the two are culturally different and in different parts of West Africa. The Empire of Gana was founded by the Soninke people, whose language and culture form part of a larger ethno-linguistic group called Mande. Scholars believe that the Soninke used horses and iron technology to gradually increase their influence over their neighbors until they were in possession of an empire that stretched from the Senegal River in the west almost to the Niger River in the east.

Gana derived its wealth and power from its strategic location between the trade routes of the Sahara and the gold mines to the south. The large and populous cities of Gana were the natural stopping points for camel caravans from the north, bringing salt, manufactured goods, horses, and food through the Sahara and taking back slaves, livestock, and gold to North Africa. The Soninke were thus trading middlemen, who connected the gold mines to the Mediterranean by an overland route that went through their territory and then continued on through a treacherous, two-month journey over the Sahara Desert.

The Ganians ruled their kingdom from a city called Kumbi; modern archaeology indicates that this was probably a paved city of about 20,000 residents; this would have made it close to the same size as medieval London. The cities housed two-story buildings, markets, and eventually, large mosques. The empire was ruled by a king. Visitors to the Empire of Gana frequently remarked on the enormous wealth and diversity of the kingdom's economic resources. If contemporary reports are to be believed, the King of Gana could field an extremely large army by contemporary standards. He paid for his administration largely by taxing the goods that were traded in the empire and extracting resources from gold mines under royal control. He also served as the chief administer of justice in the realm.[24]

Religion in the Empire of Gana

Before the coming of Islam, the Soninke people practiced traditional animistic religions; that is, they reverenced the spirits that they saw operating in the forces of nature. Instances of these beliefs appear in *Gassire's Lute* in the form of talking animals and musical instruments that play by themselves. The focus of this religion seems to have centered on worship accomplished in sacred groves, which regularly involved the use of what later Muslim writers would call "idols", that is sacred objects. Interestingly, priests were usually drawn from the class of blacksmiths, who possessed the secret knowledge required to create these sacred objects. We will see an echo of these animistic beliefs in the creation of Gassire's lute itself, which becomes a sacred object forged by a blacksmith and then *animated* by the life force of his dead sons.

However, as a trading empire, the Soninke people came into regular contact with Muslims from North Africa, who at first lived in their own separated cities. Ganian rulers found the knowledge of Muslims useful in the administration of the empire, and intermixing gradually began to occur. In the 11th century, a fundamentalist Islamic group known as the Almoravids achieved power and spread their influence throughout the Sahel, generating more converts to Islam. By the time of the Songhay Empire, Islam had become the official state religion; most of the kings of the Malian and Songhay Empire both practiced Islam and patronized the religion.[25] The adoption of Islam, however, did not wipe out animism. Tensions between the traditional animistic religions of the Sahel and Islam remained, and indeed remain to this day.

---

[24] David Conrad, *Empires of Medieval West Africa*, (New York: Facts on File Inc., 2005), 17-32 and 67-82.

[25] Ibid.

Gassire's Lute

It was during the Ganian Empire that *Gassire's Lute* was first composed. It is part of the *Dausi*, the long oral epic of the Soninke people, most of which has been lost to time. The *Dausi* would have been created and preserved by griots, a hereditary office whose function was to preserve communal memory through song. Thus, the textual status of *Gassire's Lute* is strikingly similar to that of other ancient literary texts, having been initially transmitted orally and performed in public.[26] Once the oral tradition becomes written down, the text becomes "fixed." The text of *Gassire's Lute* as we have it today was recorded relatively late, transmitted by outsiders. The most current English translation by Alta Jablow is based on a German prose text, the original having been lost to time and the impermanence of orality. To quote Jablow:

> *Gassire's Lute* was recorded in 1909 by Leo Frobenius, the German anthropologist. He heard it from a bard in Northern Dahomey, who claimed descent from the original family of Soninke bards that had migrated from the west a century before. . . . (Frobenius nowhere includes the native text, nor gives any inkling of what it was like).[27]

It is vital for us to realize that while the text of *Gassire's Lute* is reconstructed from imperfect witnesses, this feature is common to classical texts. The premodern textual world is often one reconstructed by literary historians, regardless of continent of origin.

The action of *Gassire's Lute* is framed by poetic accounts of Wagadu, the main city-state of the medieval Kingdom of Gana. Note the cycle of rising and falling found in the opening and closing frames of the poem. Why is this cycle important? What do the people of Wagadu gain from patterns of destruction and rebirth?

---

[26] The Homeric *Iliad* and *Odyssey* were developed in the same manner, over the course of centuries.

[27] *Gassire's Lute*, 9

42

Note too that Wagadu has been through four phases: the fifth is yet to come, and will differ radically from the others. This anticipation of a fifth Wagadu actually could serve as evidence for the antiquity of the text: the Soninke people would convert to Islam in the Middle Ages, but this text shows no direct or even oblique reference to Muslim belief and practice. As such, its cosmology and imagination reveal the mind of African artists before contact with Abrahamic religions, a truly "classical" African epic. The frame also includes markers of the oral, performed nature of the poem, found in the outcries in the text: "Hoooh! / Dierra, Agada, Gana, Silla! / Hoooh Fasa!" (15-16). The performer of the epic is addressing the audience directly, singing or exhorting them to pay attention to the content of the poem.[28]

Gassire's Lute records the story of the first fall of Wagadu, through vanity, and Gassire himself partakes of the tropes of both *hybris* and heroism typically associated with tragic and epic heroes in the Western tradition. Pay attention to the *ethos* of Gassire. What does he desire? What motivates him? What is the central problem faced by Wagadu? Notice that the turning point of Gassire's desire in the epic is when he finds the possibility of fame and immortality through poetry. Kiekorro, a wise old counsellor, opines that "fate will lead [Gassire] to the guinea hens in the field" (20), and that this fate will make Gassire into a bard, and will cause the downfall of Wagadu. Like Oedipus or Creon denying Tiresias (*Oedipus Rex*, *Antigone*), Gassire denies Kiekorro: "Your vision is false, / And you are a fool".[29] Gassire wanders away alone from the post-battle revelry of the warriors to the fields, where he hears a guinea hen singing a great epic poem, the *Dausi*:

---

[28] These exclamatory interjections at various points in the epic recall similar performative traces in Western epic, such as Homeric invocations to the muse, the opening "Hwæt!" of *Beowulf*, or performance-based marginalia in MS Digby 23, one of the most important witnesses to *The Song of Roland*.

[29] *Gassire's Lute*, ed. and trans. Alta Jablow, 20.

"Hear the Dausi!
Hear my deeds!"
The guinea hen sang of its battle with the snake.
The guinea hen sang:
    "All creatures must die, be buried, and vanish.
    Kings and heroes die, are buried, and vanish.
    I, too, shall die, shall be buried, and vanish.
    But the Dausi,
        The song of my battles,
        Shall not die.
    It shall be sung again and again.
    It shall outlive all kings and heroes.
    Hoooh! That I might do such deeds!
    Hoooh! That I might sing the Dausi!
    Wagadu will be lost,
    But the Dausi shall endure and live!"[30]

Immortality is what drives Gassire to attempt to learn the *Dausi*, the long epic poem of the Soninke people.[31] Once Gassire's heart is set on poetic immortality, the fate of Wagadu is sealed. Though he is warned of the consequences of his actions, Gassire denies them in an act of defiance worthy of any tragic or epic hero: "Then let Wagadu be lost![32] Gassire, however, faces a problem: how does he go about making his lute able to sing? Look at the words of the smith from 29-30—is Gassire's interpretation of his instructions accurate or not?

---

[30] Ibid., 24.

[31] The equation of immortality with poetic fame is a common feature of the ancient Greek tradition. As Gregory Nagy notes, relating to Achilleus in the *Iliad*: "The hero, the story of the hero, cannot be complete if he lives on. For in death the hero wins the ultimate prize of life eternal in song." (*The Ancient Greek Hero in 24 Hours*, 0.42: https://chs.harvard.edu/CHS/article/dispaly/5891). Gassire's desires show that it is present in the Soninke people of premodern Africa as well.

[32] Gassire's Lute, 27.

What do you make of the moral dilemma Gassire faces, and his response to it?

The conclusion of *Gassire's Lute* is ambiguous. The people of Wagadu can no longer tolerate his actions, and banish him to the desert. Only there, in the desert, does the lute begin singing the *Dausi* (37). The timing of this song, and Gassire's response, are significant: what happens at the same time as the song? The audience is left to wonder at Gassire's reaction: why exactly does he weep at this moment? The text does not answer these questions unambiguously, but like any good classical text, they form the basis for audience discussion and debate. *Gassire's Lute* stands next to the classical epic or tragedy in its plot, character, and thought, and it may be worth considering whether Gassire is a more tragic or epic figure: does his story lead you to pity him, admire him, or something of both?

Finally, it is important to note that *Gassire's Lute* is an artistic artefact of a living tradition. The *griots* of West Africa preserve the musical traditions of their ancestors, demonstrating the persistence of a millennia-old song culture in contemporary West Africa. The classical imagination is, to a certain extent, still alive in West Africa. This tradition also had an American expression as well: the American banjo is nothing more than a West African gourd lute, like the one played by Gassire. Enslaved Africans brought this instrument and their rich musical traditions to America, and West African music would go on to profoundly shape the music of the United States, from folk to blues to jazz to hip-hop to Rock N' Roll. Even in the face of horrific oppression, the West African musical culture persisted and transformed American culture. Perhaps the fifth Wagadu, the one that lives in the heart and that will never die, is among us even now.

Part-Two

The Monotheistic Imagination

One of the most significant shifts in the classical imagination was from imagining divinity as a plurality to imagining divinity as a unity. The worship of gods and the imaginative horizons they occupied stressed their plurality of characters and influences. Not so for a monotheist. While early Jewish people appeared to believe that gods besides YHWH existed, there was no doubt in their mind that *their* God was the ultimate God. Over time, Judaism became the first major monotheistic religion: the God of Judaism was the *only* God, and all other divinities were either lies (at best) or demonic beings. Consider Exodus: the Lord goes out of his way to stress that his people, the Jewish people, are not to worship any false idols. This is a huge step for the imagination: it is one thing to worship your own god while acknowledging others; it is quite another thing to deny that any God actually exists besides your own.

The great monotheistic, Abrahamic religions (Judaism, Christianity, and Islam) would profoundly alter the classical imagination. For one thing, as they spread they introduced an element of doubt into traditional habits of thought and practice: your ancestors may have worshiped idols, but these faiths called you to worship the One True God. While knowledge of divinity in polytheism relied on old, oral tradition, knowledge of God in the Abrahamic faiths had definite written sources: the Hebrew Bible, the Christian Testament, and the Quran, all of which were revealed by God Himself. Though gods might favor regions or peoples, the God of monotheism is also a *personal* God, desiring a relationship with each human person. This was a step towards a more modern understanding of the individual human person (even the term "person" was coined by Christian theologians). Perhaps most importantly, the Abrahamic tradition introduced the notion of progress. In the first place, one could point to a time before one's conversion to the true faith and the time afterwards: either as an individual or as a civilization, you could now divide time into "before revelation" and "after revelation." More importantly, all Abrahamic religions posit a definite creation of this world and a definite end of this world; the cyclical view of time would be replaced with a progressive one. Monotheism continues to shape the imagination of cultures across the globe, and continues to serve as a sort of bridge between the classical world and our world.

Chapter Six

The Hebrews: From Abraham to Jesus

By Gregory Murry

Our own culture in the western world owes a debt to the Hebrews, whose contribution to the Origins of the West primarily consists of a series of related spiritual insights, which reveal that the universe is created and ruled by one, all-powerful and loving God, who desires a personal relationship with his human creations, commands specific forms of moral behavior, and intervenes in history to save his chosen people. The Christian interpretation further claims that this God is triune in nature and became incarnate in the historical person of Jesus Christ, who died on the cross in expiation for humanity's sins.

The root of these spiritual insights occurred around 1800 BC, more than a millennium before the founding of Rome and more than 1300 years before the Golden Age of Athens. Jesus was born sometime between 7 BC and 4 AD in what is present-day Israel, during the reign of Augustus. After Jesus' state-ordered execution, the Christian faith illegally spread throughout the Roman world until it was finally legalized by the Emperor Constantine in 313 AD. By the fall of the Roman Empire in the West, Christianity was the dominant religion, and it has continued to hold great sway over the lives and imaginations of many people to this day.

Abraham and the Covenant with Yahweh

The Hebrew people trace their lineage to a shepherd named Abraham, who migrated out of Ur (probably present-day Iraq) and into present-day Israel, probably around 1800 BC. The stories told about Abraham in Genesis stress the covenant made between himself and his god, Yahweh.[33] In exchange for Abraham's faith, Yahweh promised to make Abraham's descendants as numerous as the stars and give them Israel for their inheritance. Unlike other near eastern civilizations, the Hebrews did not establish a great empire. The earliest Hebrews were nomads notable primarily for their refusal to intermarry with neighboring tribes and for their devotion to one particular God, for whom they practiced circumcision as a sign of the covenant. Though Abraham never established an empire, his descendants were certainly numerous: Islam, Judaism and Christianity all regard Abraham as the father of their religion.

Joseph and the Migration to Egypt

According to the book of Genesis, Abraham's wife conceived a child in her old age, whom they named Isaac. Isaac begat Jacob, and Jacob had twelve sons, the most beloved of whom he called Joseph. Joseph's jealous brothers sold him into slavery into Egypt, where he eventually rose to a position of prominence due to his ability to successfully interpret the pharaoh's dreams.

According to the Book of Exodus, the pharaohs eventually enslaved the Hebrews. After 400 years of slavery, the Hebrews were led out of Egypt by a man named Moses, who brought them to the land of Israel.

---

[33] Jewish people traditionally do not pronounce the name of God. Rather than say Yahweh, they say Adonai (Lord) whenever it occurs in a Hebrew text.

The Kingdom of David and the Assyrian Invasion

The Bible recounts that after the flight from Egypt, the Hebrews came into conflict with the Philistines, a group of seafaring people who arrived in Israel/Palestine around the same time. In modern times, the question of who got there first has become a life or death struggle, as Israelites and Palestinians have waged almost continuous war over the territory since the establishment of the modern state of Israel in 1948.

At first, the Hebrews were ruled by judges. In the eleventh century BC, they elected a king named Saul, whose place was eventually taken by David. David united all the Hebrew tribes under his monarchy and established a capital in Jerusalem. His son Solomon built a temple in Jerusalem to house the Ark of the Covenant and the Ten Commandments. As part of the covenant with Yahweh, David was promised a kingship that would last forever.

Initially, the Hebrews thought this meant that their political kingdom would last forever; this assumption was only strengthened when the ten northern tribes broke away in 930 BC and then were defeated and scattered by the Assyrian Empire in 722 BC. The tribe of Judah remained loyal to the house of David, and they were miraculously spared. The Jews naturally interpreted this as a sign that as long as a member of the House of David ruled, God would not allow them to be conquered.

The Babylonian Captivity

This interpretation of the covenant was put to the test less than two hundred years later, when the Jews were defeated by the Babylonian Empire and taken into captivity for several decades (597-539 BC). During this time, the Jews maintained their distinctive identity, explaining their defeat in a relatively unique way for the time: that is, they assumed that the Babylonian Captivity was Yahweh's punishment for their own lapses in maintaining the covenant, rather than assuming that the Babylonian gods had defeated Yahweh. The Babylonian Captivity ended when Cyrus the Great[34] of Persia defeated the Babylonians and allowed the Jews to return to their homeland.

The Experience of Occupation

When Jesus was born, Palestine was under the rule of the Roman Empire. Foreign domination was nothing new to the Jews; after the end of the Babylonian Captivity, they were successively conquered by the Persians, the Macedonian Greeks, and finally the Romans, who pacified Palestine when the armies of Pompey the Great conquered it in 63 BC. Indeed, the King Herod of the nativity story was a client-king of Rome who owed his power to his alliance with Marc Antony. When Antony was defeated at Actium, Herod cast his lot in with Augustus, who had fully consolidated his power over the Roman Empire at the time of Jesus' birth. For the Jews, the expected Davidic political kingdom had not materialized.

Tensions in Jewish Society

At the time of Jesus' birth, Jewish society was rife with tensions, especially between those Jews who had adopted the customs of their foreign occupiers and those who wanted to maintain a distinctive Jewish identity. After the Babylonian Captivity, most Jews had started speaking Aramaic, the language of their captors. Thus, Jesus would have primarily spoken Aramaic, though he would have also known Hebrew.[35] Other Jews had adopted the Greek language and Greek customs. Jesus probably spoke some Greek as well. Indeed,

---

[34] Cyrus the Great was the grandfather of Xerxes, the Persian king who invaded Greece in 480 BC.

[35] In his human nature, at least, he almost certainly did not know Latin (apologies to Mel Gibson). Sean Lewis footnote.

almost all of the New Testament (with the possible exception of the Gospel of Matthew) was originally written in Greek.

Moreover, there were some Jews who collaborated with the Romans, like the tax collectors and wealthy temple class of priests known as the Sadducees, whose interpretation of Judaism clashed with the more popular Pharisees, a group who insisted on strict adherence to the law and rejected the legitimacy of Gentile authorities. On the margins of society lived another group, the Essenes, who shared goods in common and practiced celibacy, much like the early Christian communities. Finally, Jewish society was awash in political turmoil, as several hardline nationalist groups known as zealots longed to eject the pagan Romans from Palestine and were constantly plotting rebellion.[36]

Galilee

Jesus was born to a woman named Mary and raised in Nazareth, a small town in Galilee. Galilee was an agricultural region in the north, quite outside the mainstream currents of Jewish life in the south. However, there were several Roman roads through southern Galilee, and the area was particularly prone to political instability and social banditry. Many of Jesus' earliest disciples, such as Peter and Andrew, were fishermen who worked on the Sea of Galilee. During the time of Christ, the region was awash in false messiahs, who attracted large followings by promising political liberation from the Romans. The Romans, as we might expect, brutally suppressed these movements and typically executed the leaders. From the Roman point of view, the miracle-working Jesus from Galilee might have looked quite a lot like a great many other such figures.

---

[36] Much of our information about Jewish society in the first century comes from Flavius Josephus, a Jewish leader and Roman collaborator. See Josephus, *The Jewish War*, trans. G.A. Williamson (London: Penguin, 1981).

Chapter Seven

The Spread of Christianity

By Gregory Murry

When the western empire fell to Germanic invasions in the fifth century, much of the old order went with it. Towns cleared out, population declined, and the art of letters decayed. Fortunately for the West, the late Roman age had already built the ark that would carry classical civilization through this flood: when the western empire fell, much of the heritage of the classical world would be entrusted to the Christian church to keep alive.

Christianity and the Roman Persecutions

From one perspective, the rise of Christianity is rather difficult to explain. Indeed, for the first three centuries, Christianity's primary marketing tool was the promise of a grisly execution at the hands of Roman authorities. Nevertheless, the Christian religion made steady converts, and by the fall of the Roman Empire in the West, Christianity was the dominant religion in the Roman world.

Before Christianity achieved this position, however, Christians suffered nearly three centuries of persecution. The first persecution occurred around 64-67 AD under the emperor Nero, who falsely accused the Christians of Rome of setting fire to the city, rounded up as many as he could find, and then subjected them to the most gruesome tortures that his perverse Roman mind could imagine. The charge for which they were punished, according to one Roman historian, was "hating the human race."[37]   According to Christian tradition, both Peter and Paul were martyred in Rome during Nero's persecutions; the churches of Saint Peter's Basilica and Saint Paul's Outside the Walls are thought to be built over their respective graves.

In spite of Nero's sadism, persecution was not constant. Some early Roman Emperors followed a don't ask, don't tell policy towards Christianity. However, as the new religion continued to spread, the Roman Emperors became steadily more alarmed, mainly because the Christian communities refused to worship the emperor as a god, but also because of rumors suggesting that Christians met secretly to engage in ritualistic cannibalism (probably due to a garbled account of the Eucharist).[38]   By the third century, Christianity was being persecuted all across the Roman world.

Yet in spite of that, or perhaps because of it, the new religion continued to expand. Christianity had its advantages over the Roman world. By many accounts, Romans of the imperial age were desperately seeking a religion that could offer more than the state-sponsored imperial cult. Indeed, Christianity was not the only near-eastern religion making converts. The Persian religion of Mithraism and the Egyptian Isis cult, which both appeared similar to Christianity in many respects, made many converts too.

Christians had other advantages. They practiced pacifism, avoiding the violence that permeated the rest of Roman culture. They preached spiritual equality between the sexes. They forbid infanticide and abortion. Perhaps most importantly, they held goods in common and took care of the poor, sick, and needy. As a result, the new religion was popular amongst those whom traditional Roman society had disregarded and oppressed: the urban poor, the

---

[37] Tacitus, *Annals of Imperial Rome* (London: Penguin, 1996), 365.

[38] Justin Martyr, *The First and Second Apologies*, trans. Leslie William Barnard (New Jersey: Paulist Press, 1997), 41.

enslaved, and the female. By the fourth century, nearly one-fifth of the Roman world had converted to Christianity.[39]

One of the turning points in this story occurred in the year 312 AD, when the emperor of the western half of the Roman Empire, a man named Constantine, affixed a Christian symbol to his battle standards and defeated a rival emperor just outside of Rome at the Battle of Milvian Bridge. The following year, Constantine legalized the Christian religion, thereby ending the era of persecution.

Constantine was the first emperor to take a leadership role in the Christian Church. He believed that the emperor should play an active role in church leadership and help to resolve doctrinal controversies. Constantine thus opened up new questions about the relationship between the Christian church and the state, questions that still remain contentious today.

Christianity and the Classical Tradition in the Patristic Age

In the third century, one important Christian thinker named Tertullian famously asked "What has Athens to do with Jerusalem?" By this he was questioning whether the Christian faith had any use for Greek philosophy. Tertullian thought that Athens had very little to do with Jerusalem, but his was a minority opinion. Most early Christian thinkers were convinced that faith and reason could not contradict each other, and they boldly used the language of Greek philosophy to express truths about Christianity (such as defining Jesus as the *logos*).[40] Throughout the age, Christian thinkers such as Augustine found much in Plato and Cicero that they could reconcile with Christian thought.

---

[39] See Rodney Stark, *The Rise of Christianity* (San Francisco: HarperCollins, 1997).

[40] The first Christian to articulate this idea was the Evangelist John in the opening lines of his gospel. Already by the second century, Christian apologists such as Justin Martyr were using the concept of *logos* to appeal to philosophically trained Greek and Roman audiences.

Greek philosophy was particularly important during the Christological controversies of the later patristic age, when the church fathers met at a number of ecumenical councils to settle questions about the relationship between Christ's divinity and humanity. The first council was held at Nicaea in 325 to settle the Arian controversy, which arose from a claim by a priest named Arius, who taught that Jesus Christ the son was not equal to God the father. The dispute so divided the ancient world that one observer reported that in the city of Constantinople in the early part of the fourth century:

> If you ask a man for change, he will give you a piece of philosophy concerning the Begotten and the Unbegotten; if you enquire the price of a loaf, he replies: 'the Father is greater and the Son is inferior'; or if you ask whether the bath is ready, the answer you receive is that the Son was made out of nothing.[41]

The dispute engaged such passions that at the council, Saint Nicholas (yes, that Saint Nicholas) reportedly became so enraged that he pulled Arius by his beard and punched him in the face.

To add insult to injury, Arius lost the argument. The fathers chose a Greek philosophical term (*homooúsios*, which has variously been translated as either consubstantial or 'one in being,') to describe the equality of God the father and Jesus Christ the son. The confession of faith that was drawn up at Nicaea is still recited by many Christian denominations today.

The Fall of Rome and the Conversion of the Germans

In the year 410, the unthinkable happened: the Germanic Visigoths sacked Rome. The city of Rome had not been sacked for over 600 years, and the blow was felt across the Roman Empire.

---

[41] Quoted in John Julius Norwich, *Byzantium: The Early Centuries* (London: Penguin, 1988), 139.

However, in many ways the Romans had brought it on themselves. Centuries of civil war and political corruption had finally taken their toll. Moreover, the Roman army only paid for itself when the empire was expanding; when Rome stopped expanding, the army became a drag on public finances. The Roman Empire also had increasing demographic problems, including a low birth rate and declining population; this undermined one of the traditional strengths of the Roman polity: manpower.

All this made the Roman army increasingly reliant on German auxiliaries. The Germans were only too happy to sign up, especially to escape the incursions of the even more barbaric Huns: nomads from the Asians steppes who moved into Eastern Europe during the late Imperial period. However, by this time, the Romans had lost their capacity to fully Romanize other peoples; after several decades of abuse at the hands of unscrupulous Roman governors, the Visigoths finally revolted. The Roman Emperors could only fight them with other German generals, which for obvious reasons was not a very effective strategy. In 410 AD, a Visigothic commander named Alaric marched on Rome and sacked it. A few decades later (455 AD), Rome was sacked again; the Germanic tribe that did it, the Vandals, caused so much damage to the city that their name has become a byword for wanton destruction ever since. Finally, in 476 AD, the last emperor, whose name was fittingly Augustulus (or little Augustus) was deposed by a Germanic king, thus ending the Roman Empire in the west. From there on out, Germanic kings would be in charge.

When the western half of the Roman Empire fell, Christianity again found itself evangelizing the pagan world, acting as a bridge between the classical world and the new medieval world. Literacy, for instance, was largely kept alive by monks, who laboriously hand-copied the great works of Roman culture and preserved them during this time. Just as the late Roman emperors had needed to employ Germans as auxiliaries in their military, the new German leaders needed to employ Christian Romans, especially bishops and priests, as their civil servants. The philosopher Boethius, author of the

Chapter Eight

Islam

By Sean Lewis

If you grew up in the United States of America, you almost certainly have a passing familiarity with Christianity, even if you do not hold this religion yourself. Christians have made up the majority of the U.S. population since the end of colonial era, and many Christian cultural practices continue to inform our lives (even if you are an atheist in the USA, you probably still exchange presents on Christmas). You may not be as familiar with the youngest Abrahamic religion: Islam. This brief chapter certainly won't do justice to a major global religion, and you really should learn more about it. Still, one must begin somewhere, and no educated person should be ignorant of at least the basics of the religion of over one billion people all across the world.

Islamic Beliefs

Islam focuses on revelations given to the Prophet Muhammad (unknown birth date-632). Muhammad was born in Mecca, a growing center of international trade in the Arabian Peninsula. He was orphaned as a child and raised by his uncle. Muhammad lived a fairly ordinary life until he was around 40 years of age, when he perceived a call to be the prophet for the Arab peoples. Around this time, he reported visions of the Angel Gabriel, who dictated to him the most vital document in Islam, the Quran.

In its origins, Islam clearly shares in the prophetic tradition of the other Abrahamic religions. The prophets of the Hebrew Bible (Moses, Elijah, and Isaiah, among others) played a formative role in Judaism, and they are recognized as prophets by Jewish, Christian, and Muslim believers. Furthermore, while they do not consider him to be divine, Muslims regard Jesus as one of these great prophets, second only to Muhammad.

So Muslims are monotheists who recognize and worship only a single God, Creator of the universe. They rely on the prophetic tradition stretching back to the early days of Judaism. What are some of the differences? Perhaps the most significant difference between Islam and its older siblings is found in the nature of the Muslim holy book.

The Quran

While they recognize the inspired nature of the Hebrew Bible and the Christian New Testament, the most significant text for Muslims is the Noble Quran. Muslims believe that every word of the Quran comes directly from God (Allah), transmitted through angelic revelation to Muhammad. Muhammad then dictated these revelations to several amanuenses (scribes); according to tradition, Muhammad himself was illiterate, further stressing the non-human origins of the Quran.

This is a vital point of comparison: while the Jewish and Christian scriptures grew over time, written by a variety of human writers, the Quran, in its entirety, came through Muhammad's ecstatic revelatory experiences. For Christians, Jesus Christ is the Word (John 1); for Muslims, the Quran is the Word, and they revere the Quran accordingly. Properly speaking, there exists no "translation" of the Quran, since every Arabic word is believed to have come directly from God. While English interpretations of the Quran exist (check some out!), the Quran only exists, properly speaking, in its original Arabic.

The Quran is arranged into 114 chapters (surahs), and was given its current form by Zayd ibn Thabit, one of Muhammad's personal scribes. The opening surah is frequently used in Muslim prayer, and provides an interesting parallel to Jewish and Christian scriptural traditions:

1. Bismillaah ar-Rahman ar-Raheem
2. Al hamdu lillaahi rabbil 'alameen
3. Ar-Rahman ar-Raheem Maaliki yaumid Deen
4. Iyyaaka na'abudu wa iyyaaka nasta'een
5. Ihdinas siraatal mustaqeem
6. Siraatal ladheena an 'amta' alaihim
7. Ghairil maghduubi' alaihim waladaaleen
Aameen

1. In the name of God, the Gracious, the Merciful.
2. Praise be to God, Lord of the Worlds.
3. The Most Gracious, the Most Merciful.
4. Master of the Day of Judgment.
5. It is You we worship, and upon You we call for help.
6. Guide us to the straight path.
7. The path of those You have blessed, not of those against whom there is anger, nor of those who are misguided.
Amen.[42]

How similar or different do you find this prayer from Jewish or Christian prayer traditions? While some differences might arise, this is clearly a prayer in the Abrahamic tradition of monotheism.

---

[42] *Clear Quran*, trans. Talal Itani. https://www.clearquran.com/.

Other Muslim Writings

While the Quran is obviously the most important Muslim text, there also exist other vital writings that have shaped the development of Islam:

Sunnah: an account of one of Muhammad's practices
Hadith: an account of one of Muhammad's sayings
Shariah: Muslim law

The Sunnah and Hadith help to "flesh out" the Quran: giving believing Muslims models for behavior and wisdom through the life and works of their major prophet. The focus on law further points to connections between Islam and the other Abrahamic faiths. Think back to the Ten Commandments in Exodus: Muslims have a similar regard for God's Law, such that jurists (commentators on the law) are essential figures in Islam.

The Five Pillars of Islam

From the Quran, Sunnah, Hadith, and Shariah arise the beliefs and practices of Islam, which are summarized clearly in the so-called Five Pillars of Islam, what every Muslim needs to believe and do:

1. Shahadah: confession of faith—believing that God is One, that Muhammad is his prophet, and that all that is recounted in the Quran and other Islamic writings are Sacred.

2. Salat: ritual prayer—praying five times per day (dawn, noon, afternoon, at sunset, after sunset), facing Mecca.

3. Zakat: almsgiving—giving money to the poor, determined as a percentage of one's income.

4. Sawm: fasting—abstaining from all food and drink between sunrise and sunset during the holy month of Ramadan.

5. Hajj: pilgrimage—Muslims who have the financial means to do so are required to go on pilgrimage to Mecca, specifically to pray at the Kaaba, a black stone structure that is the "House of God" for Muslims, believed to have been built by Abraham. The Kaaba also served as a pagan shrine for Arabs before Muhammad's prophecy.

Devout Muslims throughout the globe center their lives on these practices.

The Spread of Islam

Before Islam, the Mediterranean world was generally Christian, with a few major Jewish and pagan communities. Within 100 years of the founding of Islam, much of the Mediterranean world had become Muslim. How exactly did this remarkable spread occur?

Like Moses was for the Jewish people, Muhammad was not just a religious figure, but a cultural and political one. The Arabs of the Arabian Peninsula had never before been united into a single entity (rather, theirs was a tribal culture). Islam united the Arabs into a coherent cultural unit through a series of wars waged by Muhammad. When Mecca was unresponsive to his prophecy, he fled to nearby Medina where he found a following (this flight in 622—the Hegira—is year 1 on the Muslim calendar). He later returned to Mecca and conquered it, establishing Islam as the city's religion.

Muhammad had assumed that Jews and Christians would recognize him as the culmination of the Abrahamic tradition. When they didn't, Muhammad began to conquer and convert their cities and lands. Whether forced or persuaded, large numbers of people in Arabia converted to Islam. Muhammad died suddenly in 632, but had already brought the center of the Arabian world into Islam.

The Caliphs: The Origins of Sunnis and Shiites

Perhaps given the sudden nature of his death, Muhammad did not provide a clear line of succession regarding who would hold authority in Islam after him. The solution the Islamic tradition found were the caliphs, the Successors of Muhammad. Notice that that word is plural: from the beginning, there was controversy over who should take over the religious/political mantle from Muhammad.

These controversies led to the major division in Islam, between the Shiites and the Sunnis. Some Muslims thought that authority should be kept in Muhammad's family line, following his son-in-law Ali as Caliph. These Muslims were the beginnings of the Shia branch of Islam, and Shiite Muslims ("followers of Ali") make up the minority of the world's Muslims in just about every country outside of Iran (which is a Shiite country). Most Muslims favored caliphs who were not related to Muhammad, choosing to follow Muhammad's practices (Sunnah), rather than his bloodline. These Sunni Muslims make up the vast majority of the world's population of Muslims.

The Caliphates and the Spread of Islam

By the time of Muhammad's death, the Arabian Peninsula was thoroughly Muslim. The Caliphs continued to spread Islam throughout the world via military conquest, conquering new territories and spreading their faith. The Middle East, North Africa, and the Iberian Peninsula (present-day Spain and Portugal) were soon Islamic territories, ruled by various caliphates. This spread of religion via conquest might strike us as unusual, but it should be noted that Rome spread its official religion throughout the territories it conquered (though it tended to see non-Roman polytheism as simply a difference in name: the gods were the same, but with Celtic, German, Semitic, or Egyptian names). When Rome became Christian, Christianity was spread throughout the Roman world in much the same manner, but with little tolerance for other faiths (in fewer than one hundred years, Christianity went from being merely tolerated in the Empire to being the only legally-sanctioned religion, leading ultimately to the destruction of pagan temples, an end to the Olympic games, and the closing of Plato's Academy). Christianity did not convert the Roman world through military conquest, but it certainly benefitted from the prior military conquests of the Romans.

The Islamic Renaissance

Once the boundaries of the Muslim world were more or less settled, Muslim cities such as Baghdad, Iraq and Cordoba, Spain became major centers of culture and learning. Muslim scholars were particularly interested on the philosophical, mathematical, and medical texts of Greek antiquity, and these scholars wrote lengthy commentaries on the works of Plato and Aristotle, predating Christian scholastics by centuries. Arabic translations of Greek classics, in fact, helped reintroduce Aristotle to the Western world: from the early Middle Ages until the 12th century, most of Aristotle's works had been lost to Europe. Muslim scholars, however, had translated Aristotle from Greek into Syriac, then from Syriac into Arabic. Once these works were translated from Arabic into Latin, the international language of Western Europe, what happened was nothing short of an intellectual Renaissance. The thought of the High Middle Ages, the Scholasticism of the newly-invented medieval universities, would not have been possible without the Islamic Renaissance.

Islam and "The West"?

In the 700's, Christians pushed back on the Muslims, with the Byzantine Empire in the East and the nascent Frankish Empire in the West putting a halt to the Western expansion of Islam. This division between the Christian world and the Muslim world from the eighth century onward was crucial for the development of a specifically "Western" identity, beginning with Charlemagne's grandfather, Charles Martel, stopping Muslim armies in Tours, France in 732.

From the Carolingian era onwards, belonging to the "West" meant being Christian; this is why even Byzantine Christians were considered "Western," though they lived in the Eastern Mediterranean.

This development continues to have repercussions to our own time: the boundaries of Europe historically date to this original division, and to this day there are people who oppose the inclusion of Muslim countries (such as Turkey) in the European Union. Because of historical divisions, Muslims are considered by some to never be truly "Western," even when they live in Western countries. Islam is an Abrahamic religion, has appreciated Classical and Judeo-Christian heritage for centuries, and has produced holy men and women throughout the world. Nevertheless, the tension between the Christian World and the Islamic World has remained constant since the time of Charlemagne, even if it has now been translated into more secular terms. The Crusades were a messy chapter in this history, and the so-called Islamic State (ISIS) was an attempt by radical Islamists to revive the medieval Caliphate in the early 21st century. The conflict between Israelis and Palestinians, and the United States' continued involvement in Middle Eastern politics is unintelligible without this historical background. Any sociopolitical developments on a global scale need to be mindful of Islam and its rich and complicated history with Judeo-Christian civilization.

Chapter Nine

The High Middle Ages

By Gregory Murry

The term Middle Ages usually refers to the period between 500 AD and 1500 AD. This period is typically divided into three parts: the Early Middle Ages (500-1000 AD), the High Middle Ages (1000-1300 AD) and the Late Middle Ages (1300-1500 AD). The period between 500 and 800 AD is sometimes called the Dark Ages, since relatively little is known about this period compared to earlier and later ages. The High Middle Ages were marked by urbanization, increased trade, a growing population, and cultural and intellectual flourishing. In the Late Middle Ages, several catastrophes, such as the outbreak of the Black Death, checked Europe's growth.

The social structure of the Middle Ages can seem unusual to us. Rather than dividing society in social classes, medieval peoples were divided into three orders (or estates) according to the function they performed in society. The first order was comprised of the clergy, whose task was to pray. The second order was comprised of nobility, whose task was to fight and to govern. The largest order was the third order, whose job was to work. Throughout the age, most of the population consisted of peasants working the land, though by the end of the period, a sort of 'middle class' composed of artisans and other educated people had begun to emerge in urban areas.

It is important to note that the term Middle Ages was originally a derogatory label, encapsulating the perception that between the fall of the Roman Empire and the Renaissance, Western Europe had entered a cultural wasteland full of barbarism, ignorance and stupidity. According to this view, the classical and modern periods had been high marks of culture and civility; the thousand years in between was just something that happened in the middle. In some quarters this perception survives today; indeed, when something is called medieval in modern discourse, it is rarely considered a compliment.

However, this view is misleading on many counts and simply wrong on others. Medieval people were not mindless barbarians; rather, the whole era was remarkably creative, and throughout the period, medieval peoples were busy creating many of the hallmarks of our western civilization. Around 1000 AD, the situation in Europe gradually stabilized and the western world entered a period of sustained population growth, increased trade, and urbanization, which historians call the High Middle Ages.[43] Much of this growth was stimulated by new agricultural techniques that allowed the West to grow more food than it had in previous centuries. Foremost among these were crop rotation and the heavy plow.

The Rise of Cities

As the countryside filled up, the excess population started to find its way to cities and towns. By comparison with modern cities, these medieval towns were still quite small; many cities housed no more than 5,000 people, which for comparative purposes is about the size of Thurmont. Even the large cities were not large by our standards;

---

[43] Most of the information for this chapter comes from Brian Tierney and Sidney Painter, *Western Europe in the Middle Ages, 300-1475*, sixth edition (Boston: McGraw Hill, 1999).

in the year 1200, London probably had a population of around 20,000, which is about the size of Westminster, Maryland.[44]

As cities started to grow, local rulers would grant them liberties and the privilege to dispense their own justice. Cities became centers for the production of goods made by artisans such as smiths, coopers, and cobblers. These groups often joined together in fraternal, occupation-based protection societies known as guilds. In some cities, such as medieval Florence, the guilds eventually took full political control of the city and restarted Western civilization's experimentation with republican forms of rule.[45] In other places, cities would hold great fairs that brought buyers and sellers together, thus stimulating trade and the development of a money economy, as well as providing burgeoning political lords with a new source of revenue.

The growth of trade was also stimulated by other factors. Indeed, when they weren't busy raping, pillaging, and plundering, the Vikings of the north were busy moving goods around in their shallow drafted boats. Moreover, once European knights began going on crusade after 1095, they often returned with a taste for the luxury goods of the east, such as silk, spices, and later, porcelain.

The Medieval University

Interaction with the Near East and Medieval Spain also brought Western Europe into contact with the most highly advanced civilization of the age: the Islamic World. Islam proved a powerful unifying force for the warlike Arabian tribes, who broke out of their traditional lands and took over many of the old parts of the eastern Roman Empire. By the age of Charlemagne, they were already well entrenched from the Middle East to the Iberian Peninsula. In contrast

---

[44] Gwyn Williams, *Medieval London* (Oxon: Routledge, 2007), 317.

[45] See John Najemy, *Corporatism and Consensus in Florentine Electoral Politics, 1280-1400* (Chapel Hill: University of North Carolina Press, 1982).

to Europe, the Islamic world was heavily urbanized; for instance, during Charlemagne's time, Baghdad boasted a population of over a million people.

Islamic civilization thus inherited the treasures of Greek culture and philosophy, and the European West was largely reintroduced to Greek science and philosophy (such as Aristotle) through contemporary Islamic civilizations, particularly that of Muslim Spain, which housed by far the largest library in the West.

Much of this new learning centered on a new institution: the university, which developed out of cathedral schools. Students in the medieval university began their studies with the trivium: a course of studies comprised of grammar, logic, and rhetoric. Students then progressed to four subjects known as the quadrivium: astronomy, arithmetic, geometry, and music (which in the Middle Ages usually involved a lot of math, but not necessarily any singing or instruments).[46] After mastering the liberal arts (literally, the arts that are worthy of free people), students could enter specialized training for careers in medicine, law, or theology; indeed, the demands for legal expertise were ever-growing in an increasingly complex, commercial medieval society.

However, throughout the Middle Ages, theology remained the most prestigious degree awarded by universities; it was called the queen of the sciences because its subject matter was considered the most important. Throughout much of the period, scholastic theologians such as Thomas Aquinas were hard at work trying to reconcile the truths they found in Aristotle with the Christian faith.

---

[46] Hunt Janin, *The University in Medieval Life, 1179-1499* (Jefferson, NC: McFarland, 2008), 45-46.

Chapter Ten

Medieval Literature

By Sean Lewis

An Introduction to Medieval Literature

"Medieval literature" is an almost embarrassingly broad term compared to other periods of Western literary history. Renaissance literature is generally considered to span from the fourteenth through the early seventeenth centuries, and Romantic literature (by a very strict definition) was the product of only about 30 years of intense poetic activity around the year 1800. Modern literature is usually considered in terms of national linguistic groups: this is why Mount St. Mary's has professors of English, Italian, and Spanish. In contrast to modern periods and divisions, medieval literature spans about 1000 years (from the sixth century to the sixteenth century, in its broadest definition), and major works composed before the collapse of the Western Roman Empire should be considered "medieval" in terms of their influence: St. Augustine's *Confessions* and Boethius' *Consolation of Philosophy* are two such texts that were "best sellers" throughout the Middle Ages, shaping the literary imagination of poets and audiences. Medieval literature is preand transnational, being produced before the national and linguistic divisions that we take for granted; the English and French courts of the twelfth century were intertwined, and the works of poets like

Chrétien de Troyes and Marie de France circulated on both sides of the English Channel. Perhaps most significantly, medieval literature is multilingual: the main division in the medieval imagination was between literature written in Latin (the universal language of Western Europe and Catholic Christendom) and literature written in various vernaculars (the non-Latin languages that grew up in the Middle Ages, such as French, Italian, Spanish, German, English, Danish, and Polish). Stories were told and retold back and forth across linguistic divisions; the Arthurian legend, for example, is transmitted in texts composed in Latin, Welsh, French, English, Old Norse, Italian, Provençal, German, Spanish, and Russian![47] Given the temporal, spatial, and linguistic range of medieval literature, it is all the more surprising that there is so much common ground among the great variety of literary works produced in the period. This chapter serves as only a brief introduction to the subject,[48] but medieval literature is best understood in terms of its production, circulation, and performance and its relationship to the Bible and classical Latin works; both of these features account for the ways in which medieval literature was read and interpreted and why, in contrast to ancient and modern literature, medieval literature displays a greater variety of genres. All of these features should be kept in mind as we read *The Divine Comedy*.

Production, Circulation, and Performance

If you were the Abbess of Whitby in Northern England around the year 700, how would you go about getting a book? In the first place, you would need to know what book you wanted; book stores began to pop up in the later Middle Ages, but at this time no such

---

[47] *The Romance of Arthur: An Anthology of Medieval Texts in Translation*, ed. James J. Wilhelm (New York and London: Garland Publishing, Inc., 1994), vii.

[48] For a more comprehensive introduction, see C. S. Lewis, *The Discarded Image: An Introduction to Medieval and Renaissance Literature* (Cambridge: Cambridge University Press, 1964).

places existed; there was no such thing as browsing bookstore aisles. As a result, you would only desire a book that you had heard about or had encountered at another place, perhaps on a visit to another abbey. Suppose that you, Abbess Hilda of Whitby, had a conversation with Br. Bede from Wearmouth Abbey, in which he mentioned that his monastery had a copy of St. Augustine's *City of God*, a text you had heard of but never read (there being no copy in your own abbey). The first thing you would have to do is ask Br. Bede, in Christian charity, if his abbey would lend you their copy; supposing that Bede was a saintly man, he would agree, and Wearmouth's *City of God* would arrive at your abbey.

The next thing you would do is kill a flock of sheep. That is not a joke. Until the introduction of paper to Europe in the thirteenth century, all books were written on vellum, the scraped, tanned, stretched, and bleached skin of animals; even after paper came along, vellum continued to be the material of choice for book production (the first printed book in Western history, the Gutenberg Bible of 1455, was printed on vellum). Once the vellum had been prepared (a long and laborious process), it was then pricked and ruled. Using a knife and pen, a member of the scriptorium (the place in the monastery in which books were copied) would craft the "layout" of the page (ruled notebook paper is a modern descendant of this process). Then the copying would begin: workers in the abbey's scriptorium would divide up the text and copy Augustine's words, line by line, on sheets of vellum. This process, as you can imagine, was incredibly time consuming and hard on the monks: medieval marginalia (notes in the margins) survive that say things like, "This work is done; thank God: my hand really hurts." If you wanted your text illuminated with beautiful pictures, then artists would draw them in spaces reserved on the page. After the entire text was copied, the bunches of vellum would be stitched together and bound to a binding of wood, leather, and sometimes metal. After that, you would have your own copy of Augustine's *City of God*.

This process of making books should indicate that books in the Middle Ages were *expensive*. Over the course of the Middle Ages, book production in monasteries was eventually overtaken by scriptoria operating at universities like Paris and Oxford, as well as scriptoria run by cathedrals (Paternoster Row by St. Paul's in London was a major center of book production from the Middle Ages well into the modern era). The university and cathedral scriptoria made book production faster and cheaper than it had been at the beginning of the period, but books remained costly throughout the Middle Ages. As a result, the number of medieval people who could read was far below modern literacy rates, and readers in the early Middle Ages tended to be clergy, who needed to read for liturgical and homiletic reasons. Over the course of the centuries, members of the upper classes became literate (although it was a luxury; you don't need to read to be an effective baron or knight), and by the end of the Middle Ages, members of the middle class were a major market for vernacular literature.[49]

It would be a mistake, however, to think that medieval literature was available only to those who could read: medieval literature was performed orally, to an audience. Geoffrey of Vinsauf, in his *Poetria Nova* (a writer's manual for poetry), exhorts thirteenth-century poets to consider the memory and delivery of their poetry, as well as its matter, arrangement, and style: poets and audience alike thought in terms of oral performance. This point cannot be stressed enough: even medieval people who could not read themselves could be read *to*, and a single literate person could perform a work for a great number of listeners. Some of the most famous medieval works, such

---

[49] It is also important to note that "literate" meant something different in the Middle Ages: the ability to read and write *in Latin*; by medieval standards, many of the *professors* at Mount St. Mary's are illiterate (don't tell the Advancement Office!). When professionals in the middle class began to read and write in their respective vernaculars (being able to keep records, for example, is a great help if you are running a business!), they were still not considered "literate" if they could not read and write in Latin. This middle class still wanted to read, and a market opened up for books translated from Latin into various vernaculars and for newly composed vernacular works.

as *Beowulf* and *The Song of Roland*, display features that indicate that they were developed out of an oral tradition and were intended to be read (or chanted) to an audience. Medieval literature, then, is aural and communal; it is not meant to be read alone, silently, in a dorm room. Of course, the most important book (*books*, really)[50] of the Middle Ages would have been heard daily, chanted in Latin, in the thousands of churches and monasteries across Europe.

The Bible, the Classics, and Medieval Reading

Three seconds of searching on Mount St. Mary's Library website will turn up several books on the Bible in the Middle Ages; this is not simply because we are a Catholic university with its own seminary. The Bible was *the* book of the Middle Ages, considered to be the inspired word of God, one of the central instruments of divine revelation. If you could read at all in the Middle Ages, you read the Bible. The most prevalent translation of scripture throughout the Middle Ages was the Vulgate of St. Jerome, the standard Latin edition for over 1500 years. The Bible was read slowly, aloud, in company; this slow reading encouraged *lectio divina*, the practice of ruminating on the words of scripture much like a cow chews its cud (that image is directly from the Middle Ages). As readers and listeners masticated the words, chewed them over in their minds and imaginations, they connected different parts of scripture with one another and considered the non-literal meanings of the texts. This process of reading, listening, and interpreting led to two vital medieval interpretive practices: typology and fourfold exegesis.

If you are Christian, you have encountered typology before, possibly without knowing it. Medieval readers interpreted the Bible with the Bible; hearing one line of scripture would bring to mind five

---

[50] "Bible" comes from the Greek *ta biblia*, "the books." It becomes a singular noun only when it is translated into Latin (Biblia, Bibliae), then modified into various vernacular languages: Bible, Biblia, Bibbia, Bibel, Bijbel, библия, etc.

others, from five different places, that use the same language or have the same subject.[51]   As a result, different parts of the Bible were considered to be "types" of other parts.   The most significant types were sections in the Old Testament (Hebrew Bible) that were seen as prefigurations of Christ's Incarnation and Redemption, recounted in the Christian New Testament.   Abraham sacrificing his son Isaac (Genesis 22) became an "antetype" for God sacrificing his Son Jesus Christ on the cross (Matthew 27, Mark 15, Luke 23, John 19): Isaac carries up a mountain the bundle of wood on which he will be sacrificed like a lamb, and God's miraculous intervention prevents Isaac from dying.   Parallels between Old Testament antetypes and New Testament types abound in the sermons and art of the Middle Ages, and remain part of the Christian tradition.   If you visit the Mount's Basilica of the Immaculate Conception (the big church beneath the giant golden statue of Mary), you'll see on the pendatives of the dome (the vaguely triangular sections supporting the central dome) pictures of a youth, a lion, an ox, and an eagle.   These are the symbols of the four evangelists (Matthew, Mark, Luke, and John, respectively), and are taken from the Old Testament book of Ezekiel 1:10: the faces of the terrifying "living creatures" have been and continue to be interpreted as antetypes of the evangelists.   On the southern rose window, you'll also see the Ark of the Covenant as a name applied to Mary: just as the ark in Exodus 36 contained the Glory of God, so Mary contained God Himself inside her body. Examples of Christian typological reading are almost endless.

From these endless typologies, it is clear that medieval readers were not considering scripture only in its literal sense: biblical literalism is an invention of the modern world, not the medieval.   St.

---

[51] It would be accurate to say that the greatest medieval Biblical readers were living concordances of the Bible. A biblical concordance is a book that lists all the times specific words are mentioned in scripture, and where they can be found.   Preachers like St. Bernard of Clairvaux had the Latin Bible essentially memorized, and could recall from memory connections based on themes, phrases, or even single words.

Augustine taught that the account of creation at the beginning of Genesis is *not* to be read literally, but rather allegorically, a fact that may surprise many 21st-century Christians and atheists alike. Scripture was considered polysemous, having several layers of meaning, and thus had to be read on many levels. These levels came to be called the fourfold method of exegesis; the thirteenth-century Dominican friar Augustine of Dacia summed it up in a little Latin jingle: "Littera gesta docet, quid credas allegoria / Moralis quid agas, quid speres anagogia": "The literal level teaches you what happened, the allegorical what you should believe; the moral what you should do, the anagogical what you should hope for." While all readers of medieval literature should have these lines memorized and/or tattooed on them, they do require some explaining. By the literal level, medieval people meant the straightforward sense of the text: the plot, characters, images, etc.; on the literal level, a deer is just a deer. On the allegorical level, however, that deer contains a wealth of signification and hidden meaning. Consider this allegorical reading of a deer from a thirteenth-century bestiary (book about animals):

> These peculiarities [that deer support one another when crossing streams] seem to fit in with people who are devoted to the Holy Church, by a congruous and competent symbolism. For when Christians leave their pasture, i.e., this world, for the love of heavenly pastures, they support one another, i.e. the more perfect carry along and sustain the weight of the less perfect by their example and good works. And if they come across some occasion for sin they hurry over it at once. Also, after snuffing up the devil-snake [deer were thought to snort snakes], i.e. after the perpetration of sin, they run with Confession to Our Lord Jesus Christ, who is the true fountain, and, drinking the precepts laid down by

him, our Christians are renovated—the Old Age of Sin having been shed [like shedding antlers].[52]

That might seem far-fetched, but to the medieval imagination those allegorical levels are not mere free-association on the part of the reader, but are *actually present in the text*, and are *uncovered* by *lectio divina*. Think about that the next time you encounter a deer in the Bible (Psalm 42 anyone?). The moral level is fairly straightforward: it is the moral or ethical lesson you are supposed to learn from the text and use to live a virtuous life: like good deer shedding old antlers, Christians should shed old, sinful ways. The anagogical level is perhaps the hardest to wrap one's mind around: it is the level that reveals what life will be like after the Apocalypse, in the Heavenly Jerusalem at the end of the Book of Revelation (21-22).[53] The streams of water for which the deer longs in Psalm 42 are ultimately the streams flowing from the Heavenly Temple in Ezekiel 47, a promise of the Living Water, the Word of God, from which the blessed shall drink eternally. A skilled exegete (interpreter of texts) would read with all four of these levels constantly in mind, with the presumption that all of these meanings are *actually* in the text, unlocked by his own ruminations.

The practice of fourfold exegesis helps explain how Christians in the Middle Ages handled difficult parts of the Bible, as well as the fact that the books of the Bible comprise many different genres. In the first place, the instruction to read these works in allegorical, moral, and anagogical fashions allowed medieval readers to reconcile apparent contradictions in the Bible; if two parts seem to contradict one another or plain reason, there was always an allegorical, moral, or anagogical explanation. Moreover, medieval readers had to deal

---

[52] *The Book of Beasts*, translated by T.H. White (New York: Dover Publications, 1984 [1954]), 38-39.

[53] For some examples of Biblical texts that lend themselves to anagogical interpretation, consider Psalm 46, Isaiah 14, Zechariah 8, John 14, and 1 Corinthians 13.

with the fact that the Bible is multi-generic. In the Bible, you will find creation and foundation myths (Genesis), chronicles of Jewish political history (1 and 2 Samuel; 1 and 2 Kings), prophesies (Isaiah; Jonah), proverbial sayings (Proverbs), lyric poetry (Psalms), erotic poetry (Song of Solomon), letters to churches (most of the New Testament), and will encounter a dizzying variety of literary depictions of the natural world and the life of man. Fourfold exegesis helped tie these genres together, as well as account for some oddities. Usually we don't think about monks reading erotica, but St. Bernard of Clairvaux preached extensively on the Song of Songs, read as an allegory between God (the lover) and the Church (the beloved).

Fourfold exegesis also helps explain why and how so many classical, pagan Latin works survived and flourished in the Middle Ages. Recall that in the first few centuries of the Middle Ages, monks were the ones copying and preserving books. How could monks have read and copied tales of romantic suicide (Dido in Virgil's *Aeneid*) or advice on how to seduce women (Ovid's *Art of Love*)? While a group of particularly naughty monks might be a possible explanation, the more straightforward answer is that these classical texts were read *like the Bible was read*, with allegorical and moral lessons hiding in them. Ovid's *Metamorphoses* became extensively allegorized over the Middle Ages, and Virgil's *Aeneid* was read as an allegory of the journey of the soul to virtue. The moral philosophy of Cicero and Cato was standard grammar-school reading throughout the period, which brings up a vital point: medieval boys (and, less frequently, girls) learned their Latin grammar by reading classical texts. By the twelfth century, if you could read the Bible, you had also read Virgil, Ovid, and Cicero.

The Medieval Literary Imagination:
Dante's Divine Comedy

By now it should be clear that the literature produced by medieval authors grows out of a rich and complicated literary tradition: new works of literature were written to be performed aloud, interpreted allegorically, and considered in light of scripture and the classics. The fact that the Bible contains many genres meant that medieval poets did not make the kind of hard and fast divisions between genres that we take for granted, and often meant different things by the same terms. For instance, a "tragedy" in medieval literature is simply a story that ends sadly; a "comedy" is one that ends happily — Aristotle's finer distinctions in the *Poetics* are not used in the period. Because of its roots in biblical and classical literature, medieval literature has genres that are foreign to modern readers. These include biblical paraphrases (retellings of biblical stories), dream visions (accounts of some revelation the poet has while dreaming, often highly allegorical), beast fables (think Aesop), complaints (lamenting ill fortune; Dido is the narrator of some medieval complaints), debates (often open-ended, inviting audience participation), legends of saints, lives of saints and kings, pilgrimage narratives, *chansons de geste* (songs of knightly deeds), and romances (tales of knightly deeds mixed with courtly love). Poets like Dante and Chaucer had no qualms mixing these genres. The biblical penchant for listing items in a series (generations, plants, stones, etc.) also led to the apparently boring medieval practice of literary lists; poets will pause in the middle of a work to tell you what animals are on all of the knights' shields or how many walls a castle has and what they are made of. The joy of listing things is perhaps the weirdest part of medieval literature for modern readers.[54]

Dante called his work the *Commedia* because it ended well: the final canto of *Paradiso* gives a vision of God in heaven, which is about as happy an ending as a Christian can hope for. He had *Inferno*, *Purgatorio*, and *Paradiso* circulated as they were written, even though they form an incredibly intricate whole: numerological connections run throughout the hundred cantos (*Purgatorio* 16 and 17 mark the exact center of the *Commedia*, 16 being the last of the first 50, 17 being the first of the last 50, and the two of them sum up fairly clearly Dante's "argument" for the work as a whole). The *Commedia* is in

---

[54] See Umberto Eco, *An Infinity of Lists* (New York: Rizzoli, 2009).

Dante's vernacular (Florentine Italian), but also uses Latin and Provençal, and is in dialogue with Latin and French literature. Dante invokes the muses and the Holy Spirit to inspire him to accurately recount a pilgrimage he undertook in a vision he had while asleep (*Paradiso* 32.139). In this pilgrimage, Virgil guides him out of the dark wood in which he is trapped and then through hell and purgatory; throughout his trip, he meets figures from the Bible and from classical poetry and philosophy, as well as contemporary Italians. Virgil was sent, ultimately, by Beatrice, Dante's dead love, whom Dante loved as a courtly lover: chastely and spiritually (he was actually married to and had children with another woman). Dante the pilgrim is on an explicitly moral journey; he cannot help himself in the dark wood, so he hands his guidance to Virgil's authority: "tu duca, tu segnore e tu maestro": "you [Virgil] are my leader, my lord, and my master" (*Inferno* 2.140). Through Virgil's education in *Inferno* and through Dante's experiences in *Purgatorio*, Dante the pilgrim reaches the point at which Virgil can trust him to make his own moral decisions: "io te sovra te corono e mitrio": "I crown and miter you ruler of yourself" (*Purgatorio* 27.142). Dante's pilgrimage is not over, however, and the heavenly Beatrice leads him from pagan philosophy to Christian theology in their journey through the heavens in *Paradiso*. In the *Commedia*, Dante explicitly draws on the Bible, Virgil, Ovid, Aquinas, and Bonaventure, and his characters discuss not only the natures of sin and love, but also more apparently tangential topics, such as embryology and the nature of the dark spots of the moon. Finally, Dante instructs his readers, both in the work itself and in a letter to a friend, that the *Commedia* is to be read using the fourfold method of exegesis: he is composing the work with the intent that it be ruminated over for allegorical meaning, moral instruction, and a glimpse of what life will be like in the world to come. The *Commedia* is a masterpiece of medieval literary art, equal to Aquinas' *Summa Theologiae* or Chartres Cathedral as an expression of the medieval Catholic imagination.

Pericles' Funeral Oration

Thucydides, 431 BC

We begin our study of culture and civilization with Pericles' Funeral Oration, one of the finest pieces of rhetoric in the history of the West. Pericles delivered the oration in the first year of the Peloponnesian War, which was fought from 431-404 BC between the Athenian and Spartan alliances. The speech was recorded by Thucydides, an Athenian general, whose "History of the Peloponnesian War" is one of the first works of history. Thucydides was likely present at the funeral oration, but he admitted that when he recorded speeches, he made "the speakers say what, in [his] opinion, was called for by each situation."[55]

In the same winter, following their traditional institution, the Athenians held a state funeral for those who had been the first to die in this war. The ceremony is as follows. They erect a tent in which, two days before the funeral, the bones of the departed are laid out, and people can bring offerings to their own dead. On the day of the funeral procession coffins of cypress wood are carried out on wagons, one coffin for each tribe, with each man's bones in his own tribe's coffin. One dressed but empty bier[56] is carried for the missing

---

[55] "The Funeral Oration," from *The History of the Peloponnesian War* by Thucydides, translated by Martin Hammond, translation copyright © 2009 by Martin Hammond. Used by permission of Oxford University Press.

[56] A frame on which a coffin is transported.

whose bodies could not be found and recovered. All who wish can join the procession, foreigners as well as citizens, and the women of the bereaved families come to mourn at the grave. Their burial is in the public cemetery, situated in the most beautiful suburb of the city, where the war dead are always buried, except those who died at Marathon, whose exceptional valour was judged worthy of a tomb where they fell.

When the earth has covered them, an appropriate eulogy is spoken over them by a man of recognized intellectual ability and outstanding reputation, chosen by the city; after this the people depart. This is how they conduct the funeral: and they followed this custom throughout the war whenever there was occasion.

Over these first dead the man chosen to give the address was Pericles the son of Xanthippus. When the moment arrived he walked forward from the grave and mounted the high platform which had been constructed there so that he could be heard as far among the crowd as possible. He then spoke like this:

'Most of those who have spoken here on previous occasions have commended the man who added this oration to the ceremony: it is right and proper, they have said, that there should be this address at the burial of those who died in our wars. To me it would seem enough that men who showed their courage in actions should have their tribute too expressed in actions, as you can see we have done in the arrangements for this state funeral; but the valour of these many should not depend for credence on the chance of one man's speech, who may speak well or badly. It is not easy to find the right measure of words when one cannot quite rely on a common perception of the truth. Those in the audience who are aware of the facts and are friends of the dead may well think that the speaker's account falls short of what they know and wish to hear; and the inexperienced may be jealous, and think there must be exaggeration, if told of anything beyond their own capacity. Eulogies of others are tolerated up to the point where each man still thinks himself capable of doing something of what he has heard praised: beyond that lies jealousy and therefore disbelief. But since this institution was sanctioned and approved by our predecessors, I too must follow the custom and attempt as far as possible to satisfy the individual wishes and expectations of each of you.

'I shall begin with our ancestors first of all. It is right, and also appropriate on such an occasion, that this tribute should be paid to their memory. The same race has always occupied this land, passing it on from generation to generation until the present day, and it is to these brave men that we owe our inheritance of a land that is free. They deserve our praise. Yet more deserving are our own fathers, who added to what they themselves had received and by their pains left to us, the present generation, the further legacy of the great empire which we now possess. We ourselves, those of us still alive and now mainly in the settled age of life, have strengthened this empire yet further in most areas and furnished the city with every possible resource for self-sufficiency in war and peace. I shall not mention our achievements in war, the campaigns which won us each addition to the empire, our own or our fathers' spirited resistance to the attacks of Greek or barbarian enemies—I have no wish to delay you with a long story which you know already. But before I pass on to the praise of the dead, I shall describe first the principles of public life which set us on our way, and the political institutions and national character which took us on to greatness. I think this a suitable subject for the present occasion, and it could be of benefit for this whole gathering, foreigners as well as citizens, to hear this account.

'We have a form of government which does not emulate the practice of our neighbours: we are more an example to others than an imitation of them. Our constitution is called a democracy because we govern in the interests of the majority, not just the few. Our laws give equal rights to all in private disputes, but public preferment depends on individual distinction and is determined largely by merit rather than rotation: and poverty is no barrier to office, if a man despite his humble condition has the ability to do some good to the city. We are open and free in the conduct of our public affairs and in the uncensorious way we observe the habits of each other's daily lives: we are not angry with our neighbour if he indulges his own pleasure, nor do we put on the disapproving look which falls short of punishment but can still hurt. We are tolerant in our private dealings with one another, but in all public matters we abide by the law: it is fear above all which keeps us obedient to the authorities of the day and to the laws, especially those laws established for the protection of the injured and those unwritten laws whose contravention brings acknowledged disgrace.

'Furthermore, as rest from our labours we have provided ourselves with a wealth of recreations for the spirit—games and festivals held throughout the year, and elegantly appointed private houses, giving us a pleasure which dispels the troubles of the day. The size of our city attracts every sort of import from all over the world, so our enjoyment of goods from abroad is as familiar as that of our own produce.

'We differ too from our enemies in our approach to military matters. The difference is this. We maintain an open city, and never expel foreigners or prevent anyone from finding out or observing what they will—we do not hide things when sight of them might benefit an enemy: our reliance is not so much on preparation and concealment as on our own innate spirit for courageous action. In education also they follow an arduous regime, training for manliness right from childhood, whereas we have a relaxed lifestyle but are still just as ready as they to go out and face our equivalent dangers. I give you an example. The Spartans do not invade our land on their own, but they have all their allies with them: when we attack others' territory we do it by ourselves, and for the most part have no difficulty in winning the fight in a foreign country against men defending their own property. No enemy has yet met our full force, because we have been simultaneously maintaining our navy and sending our own men on a number of campaigns by land. If they do engage some part of our forces somewhere, a victory over just a few of us has them claiming the defeat of us all, and if they are beaten they pretend that they lost to our full strength. If then we choose to approach dangers in an easy frame of mind, not with constant practice in hardship, and to meet them with the courage which is born of character rather than compulsion, the result is that we do not have to suffer in advance the pain which we shall face later, and when we do face it we show ourselves just as courageous as those who have spent a lifetime of labour. This is one reason for the admiration of our city: and there are others too.

'We cultivate beauty without extravagance, and intellect without loss of vigour; wealth is for us the gateway to action, not the subject of boastful talk, and while there is no disgrace in the admission of poverty, the real disgrace lies in the failure to take active measures to escape it; our politicians can combine management of their domestic affairs with state business, and others who have their own work to attend to can nevertheless acquire a good knowledge of politics. We are unique in the way we regard anyone who takes no part in public affairs: we do not call that a quiet life, we call it a useless life. We are all involved in either the proper formulation or at least the proper review of policy, thinking that what cripples action is not talk, but rather the failure to talk through the policy before proceeding to the required action. This is another difference between us and others, which gives us our exceptional combination of daring and deliberation about the objective—whereas with others their courage relies on ignorance, and for them to deliberate is to hesitate. True strength of spirit would rightly be attributed to those who have the sharpest perception of both terrors and pleasures and through that knowledge do not shrink from danger.

'We are at variance with most others too in our concept of doing good: we make our friends by conferring benefit rather than receiving it. The benefactor is the firmer friend, in that by further kindness he will maintain gratitude in the recipient as a current debt: the debtor is less keen, as he knows that any return of generosity will be something owed, not appreciated as an independent favour. And we are unique in the way we help others—no calculation of self-interest, but an act of frank confidence in our freedom.

'In summary I declare that our city as a whole is an education to Greece; and in each individual among us I see combined the personal self-sufficiency to enjoy the widest range of experience and the ability to adapt with consummate grace and ease. That this is no passing boast but factual reality is proved by the very power of the city: this character of ours built that power. Athens alone among contemporary states surpasses her reputation when brought to the test: Athens alone gives the enemies who meet her no cause for chagrin at being worsted by such opponents, and the subjects of her empire no cause to complain of undeserving rulers. Our power most certainly does not lack for witness: the proof is far and wide, and will make us the wonder of present and future generations. We have no need of a Homer to sing our praises, or of any encomiast whose poetic version may have immediate appeal but then fall foul of the actual truth. The fact is that we have forced every sea and every land to be open to our enterprise, and everywhere we have established permanent memorial of both failure and success.

'This then is the city for which these men fought and died. They were nobly determined that she should not be lost; and all of us who survive should be willing to suffer for her.

'This is why I have dwelt at length on the nature of our city, to demonstrate that in this contest there is more at stake for us than for those who have no comparable enjoyment of such advantages, and also to set out a clear base of evidence to support the praise of the men I am now commemorating. Their highest praise is already implicit: I have sung the glories of the city, but it was the qualities of these men and others like them which made her glorious, and there can be few other Greeks whose achievements, as theirs do, prove equal to their praises. I consider that the way these have now met their end is the index of a man's worth, whether that be first glimpse or final confirmation. Even if some had their faults, it is right that the courage to fight and die for their country should outweigh them: they have erased harm by good, and the collective benefit they have conferred is greater than any damage done as individuals. None of these men set higher value on the continued enjoyment of their wealth and let that turn them cowards; none let the poor man's hope, that some day he will escape poverty and grow rich, postpone that fearful moment. For them victory over the enemy was the greater desire: this they thought the noblest of all risks, and were prepared to take that risk in the pursuit of victory, forsaking all else. The uncertainties of success or failure they entrusted to hope, but in the plain and present sight of what confronted them they determined to rely on themselves, and in the very act of resistance they preferred even death to survival at the cost of surrender. They fled from an ignominious reputation by withstanding the action with their lives. In the briefest moment, at the turning point of fortune, they took their leave not of fear but of glory.

'Such were these men, and they proved worthy of their city. The rest of us may pray for a safer outcome, but should demand of ourselves a determination against the enemy no less courageous than theirs. The benefit of this is not simply an intellectual question. Do not simply listen to people telling you at length of all the virtues inherent in resisting the enemy, when you know them just as well yourselves: but rather look day after day on the manifest power of our city, and become her lovers. And when you realize her greatness, reflect that it was men who made her great, by their daring, by their recognition of what they had to do, and by their pride in doing it. If ever they failed in some attempt, they would not have the city share their loss, but offered her their courage as the finest contribution they could make. Together they gave their lives, and individually they took as their reward the praise which does not grow old and the most glorious of tombs—not where their bodies lie, but where their fame lives on in every occasion for speech and ceremony, an everlasting memory. Famous men have the whole earth as their tomb. Their record is not only the inscription on gravestones in their own land, but in foreign countries too the unwritten memorial which lives in individual hearts, the remembrance of their spirit rather than their achievement.

'You should now seek to emulate these men. Realize that happiness is freedom, and freedom is courage, and do not be nervous of the dangers of war. The unfortunate, with no hope of improvement, have better reason to husband their lives than those who risk reversal of fortune if they live on and have the most to lose should they fail. To a man with any pride cowardice followed by disaster is more painful than a death which comes in the vigour of courage and the fellowship of hope, and is hardly felt.

'For that reason, to the parents of the dead here present I offer not sympathy so much as consolation. You know that you were born into a world of change and chance, where the true fortune is to meet with honour—the most honourable death for these we commemorate, the most honourable grief for you—and to enjoy a life whose measure of happiness fills both the living and the leaving of it. It is hard, I know, to convince you of this, since you will often have reminders of your sons when you see others blessed with the good fortune which was once your source of pride too: and grief is felt not for the deprivation of joys never experienced, but for the loss of a once familiar joy. Those of you who are still of an age to bear children should hold firm to the hope of further sons. In their own lives some will find that new children help them forget those they have lost, and for the city there will be double benefit—both maintenance of the population and also a safeguard, since those without children at stake do not face the same risks as the others and cannot make a balanced or judicious contribution to debate. Those of you who are past that age should consider it a gain that you have lived the greater part of your life in happiness and that what remains will be short: and you should take comfort in the glory of the dead. Love of honour alone does not age, and in the unproductive time of life the greater pleasure is not the accumulation of gain, as some say, but the enjoyment of honour.

'For those of you here who are sons or brothers of the dead I can see a formidable task. It is common experience that all speak highly of those who are gone, and however you excel in your own qualities you will struggle to be judged even a close second to them, let alone their equals. The living are exposed to the denigration of rivalry, but anything no longer present meets with warm and uncompetitive recognition.

'If I may speak also of the duty of those wives who will now be widows, a brief exhortation will say it all. Your great virtue is to show no more weakness than is inherent in your nature, and to cause least talk among males for either praise or blame.

'I have made this speech as custom demands, finding the most suitable words I could. The honour expressed in ceremony has now been paid to those we came to bury: and in further tribute to them the city will maintain their children at public expense from now until they come of age. This is the valuable crown which in contests such as these the city confers on the dead and those they leave behind. The state which offers the greatest prizes for valour also has the bravest men for citizens.

'And now it is time to leave when each of you has made due lament for your own.'

Such was the funeral held in this winter: and with the passing of winter there ended the first year of this war.

Text Two

The Plague

Thucydides, 430 BC

After recounting the Funeral Oration, Thucydides proceeds directly to this passage: a description of a plague that hit Athens in 430 BC. Note the difference between the opinions of Athens that Pericles expresses in the Funeral Oration and Thucydides' account of Athenian behavior during the plague. [57]

At the very beginning of the next summer the Peloponnesians and their allies invaded Attica, with two thirds of their forces as on the first occasion, under the command of Archidamus the son of Zauxidamus, king of Sparta. They settled in and began to ravage the land.

They had not been in Attica for more than a few days when the plague first broke out in Athens. It is said that the plague had already struck widely elsewhere, especially in Lemnos and other places, but nowhere else was there recorded such virulence or so great a loss of life. The doctors could offer little help at first: they were attempting to treat the disease without knowing what it was, and in fact there was particularly high mortality among doctors because of their particular exposure. No other human skill could help either, and all supplications at temples and consultations of oracles and the like

[57] "The Plague," from *The History of the Peloponnesian War* by Thucydides, translated by Martin Hammond, translation copyright © 2009 by Martin Hammond. Used by permission of Oxford University Press.

were of no avail. In the end the people were overcome by the disaster and abandoned all efforts to escape it.

The original outbreak, it is said, was in Ethiopia, the far side of Egypt: the plague then spread to Egypt and Libya, and over much of the king's territory. It fell on the city of Athens suddenly. The first affected were the inhabitants of the Peiraeus, who went so far as to allege that the Peloponnesians had poisoned the wells (at that time there were no fountains in the Peiraeus). Afterwards the plague reached the upper city too, and now the number of deaths greatly increased. Others, doctors or laymen, can give their individual opinion of the likely origin of the plague, and of the factors which they think significant enough to have had the capacity to cause such a profound change. But I shall simply tell it as it happened, and describe the features of the disease which will give anyone who studies them some prior knowledge to enable recognition should it ever strike again. I myself caught the plague, and witnessed others suffering from it.

It so happened that this year was commonly agreed to have been particularly free from other forms of illness, though anyone with a previous condition invariably developed the plague. The other victims were in good health until, for no apparent cause, they were suddenly afflicted. The first symptoms were a high fever in the head and reddening and inflammation of the eyes; then internally the throat and tongue began to bleed and the breath had an unnaturally foul smell. There followed sneezing and hoarseness of voice, and shortly the affliction moved down to the chest accompanied by a violent cough. When it settled in the stomach the turmoil caused there led to the voiding of bile in every form for which the doctors have a name, all this with great pain. Most then suffered from an empty retching which brought violent spasms: in some this followed as soon as the vomiting had abated, in others much later.

The surface of the body was not particularly hot to the touch or pallid, but reddish and livid, breaking out in small pustules and ulcers. But the sensation of burning heat inside the body was so strong that sufferers could not bear the pressure of even the lightest clothing or sheets, or anything other than going naked, and their greatest wish was to plunge into cold water. Many who had no one to look after them did in fact throw themselves into cisterns, overcome by an insatiable thirst: but as a rule the quantity of water drunk made no difference. A constant infliction was desperate restlessness and the inability to sleep. Throughout the height of the disease there was no wasting of the body but a surprising physical resilience to all the suffering, so that there was still some strength in them when the majority died from the internal fever after six to eight days. If they survived this period, most others died from the consequent weakness when the disease spread down to the bowels causing heavy ulceration and the onset of completely liquid diarrhea.

The disease first settled in the head then progressed throughout the whole body from the top downwards. If any survived the worst effects, symptoms appeared when the disease took hold in their extremities. It attacked genitals, fingers, and toes, and many lived on with these parts lost: some too lost their sight. There were those who on recovery suffered immediate and total loss of memory, not knowing who they were and unable to recognize their friends.

Indeed the pathology of the disease defied explanation. Not only did it visit individuals with a violence beyond human endurance, but there was also this particular feature which put it in a different category from all other diseases with which we are familiar: although many bodies lay unburied, the birds and animals which prey on human flesh kept away from them, or if they did eat, died of it. Evidence of this was the notable disappearance of carrion birds, nowhere to be seen in their usual or any other activity: the dogs, being domestic animals, allowed more immediate observation of this consequence.

This then, leaving aside the many variants in the way different individuals were affected, was the general character of the disease. Throughout this time there were no attacks of the usual illnesses: any that did occur ended in the plague.

Some died in neglect and others died despite constant care. Virtually no remedy was established as a single specific relief applicable in all cases: what was good for one was harmful to another. No particular constitution, strong or weak, proved sufficient in itself to resist, but the plague carried off all indiscriminately, and whatever their regime of care. The most dreadful aspects of the whole affliction were the despair into which people fell when they realized they had contracted the disease (they were immediately convinced that they had no hope, and so were much more inclined to surrender themselves without a fight), and the cross-infection of those who cared for others: they died like sheep, and this was the greatest cause of mortality. When people were afraid to visit one another, the victims died in isolation, and many households were wiped out through the lack of anyone to care for them. If they did visit the sick, they died, especially those who could claim some courage: these were people who out of a sense of duty disregarded their own safety and kept visiting their friends, even when ultimately the family members themselves were overwhelmed by the scale of the disaster and abandoned the succession of dirges for the dead. But the greatest pity for the dying and the distressed was shown by those who had had the disease and recovered. They had experience of what it was like and were now confident for themselves, as the plague did not attack the same person twice, or at least not fatally. These survivors were congratulated by all, and in the immediate elation of recovery they entertained the fond hope that from now on they would not die of any other disease.

The suffering was made yet more acute by the influx from the country into the city, and the incomers suffered most of all. With no houses of their own, and forced to live in huts which at that time of year were stifling, they perished in chaotic conditions: the dead and the dying were piled on top of each other, and half-dead creatures staggered about the streets and round every fountain, craving for water. The sanctuaries in which they had encamped were full of corpses—people dying there were not moved: all sacred and secular constraints came to be ignored under the overwhelming impact of the disaster, which left men no recourse. All previously observed funeral customs were confounded, and burial was haphazard, any way that people could manage. Many were driven to shameful means of disposal for lack of friends to help them, so many of their friends already dead: they made use of other people's funeral pyres, either putting their own dead on a pyre constructed by others and quickly setting light to it, or bringing a corpse to a pyre already lit, throwing it on top of the other body in the flames, and then running away.

In other respects too the plague was the beginning of increased lawlessness in the city. People were less inhibited in the indulgence of pleasures previously concealed when they saw the rapid changes of fortune—the prosperous suddenly dead, and the once indigent now possessing their fortune. As a result they decided to look for satisfactions that were quick and pleasurable, reckoning that neither life nor wealth would last long. No one was prepared to persevere in what had once been thought the path of honour, as they could well be dead before that destination was reached. Immediate pleasure, and any means profitable to that end, became the new honour and the new value. No fear of god or human law was any constraint. Pious or impious made no difference in their view, when they could see all dying without distinction. As for offences against the law, no one expected to live long enough to be brought to justice and pay the penalty: they thought that a much heavier sentence had already been passed and was hanging over them, so they might as well have some enjoyment of life before it fell.

Such was the affliction which had come on the Athenians and was pressing them hard—people dying inside the city, and the devastation of their land outside. In this time of trouble, as tends to happen, they recalled a verse which the old men said was being chanted long ago: 'A Dorian war will come, and bring a pestilence with it.' People had disputed whether the original word in the verse was *limos* ('famine') rather than *loimos* ('pestilence'): but not surprisingly in the present situation the prevailing view was that 'pestilence' was the word used. Men accommodate their memories to their current experience. I imagine that if at some time another

'Dorian war' comes after this one, with famine coinciding, the verse will in all likelihood be recited with that meaning.

Those who knew of it also remembered the oracle given to the Spartans, when they enquired whether they should go to war and the god answered that they would win if they fought in earnest, and said that he himself would take their side. The general surmise was that the facts fitted the oracle. The plague had indeed begun immediately after the Peloponnesians had invaded, and it never reached the Peloponnese to any significant extent, but spread particularly in Athens and later in other densely populated areas. So much for the facts of the plague.

Text Three

The Early History of Rome

Livy, 29-14 BC

Titus Livy was a Roman historian who was born in Padua in 59 B.C. His early years were marked by the chaos of the Roman civil wars, which he most likely witnessed first-hand. Rather than engage in politics directly, he spent much of his life composing a monumental history of Rome. It is reported that Augustus did not like Livy's political views, and it is likely that the feeling was mutual.

Livy does not write history in the way we are accustomed: indeed, his history is usually far more exciting. For one thing, Livy rarely lets the facts get in the way of a good story. For another thing, he tends to frame his narrative in episodic form, each episode meant to teach his readers a different moral about what it meant to be a good Roman, something that Livy thought was of the utmost importance given the time in which he lived.[58]

I do not know if a history on the origins of the Roman people will be worth the labor, nor if I did know, would I dare to say. Historians always believe that their work will be more definitive or well-written than previous histories, but in any case, I will enjoy studying the deeds of the world's most powerful people, and even if others outshine me, I will console myself that I am outdone by truly great and worthy writers.

This study is an immense project, as it spans more than 700 years of history, growing from small beginnings to a subject that requires enormous labor. No doubt, most of my audience will have very little

---

[58] Translation by Gregory Murry, 2014, all rights reserved.

appetite for reading about the origins of the city, and they will skip ahead to recent events, in which a once powerful people have wasted their strength in fighting each other. I, however, seek a different reward, for I will turn my attention away from the evils of our own age and return to our earliest history, completely free from those cares that might affect the soul of an historian, even if they do not deflect him from the truth.

The legends concerning the city's origin make for good stories but not for very good history (*res gestae*), and I neither want to confirm nor refute them. In order to dignify our origins, our ancestors mixed the stories of the gods with human history. Yet, if any people should be allowed to claim divine origin, the Romans should. We have won so much glory in war that other nations have little difficulty accepting our claims of divine ancestry, just as they have little difficulty accepting Roman authority itself.

However, I do not consider any of these concerns a matter of great importance; rather, I ask the reader to consider the following: what were the lives and the morals of our ancestors? With what men, what virtues, and what policies was Rome born and its empire increased? Then, let the reader see how we gradually lost our discipline and sunk into moral degeneracy. Then, let the reader see that as we slipped, we began to fall headlong into the abyss, until we reached these times, in which we are neither able to bear our vices nor apply their remedies.

Knowledge of history makes for a healthy mind because it gives us clear historical examples of every type. Thus, individuals and nations should imitate good historical examples and avoid the disgraceful ones, and unless my love for the city deceives me, there has never been a greater, more holy, or more exemplary republic than Rome. Nor has there ever been a city in which greed and luxury were so long kept away or where poverty and thrift were so long considered honorable. The fewer things the Romans had, the less greed they had. Lately, riches have stimulated greed, and large appetites have caused many to lose themselves in luxury and lust.

Nevertheless, these annoying yet necessary criticisms should not grace the preface of such a work. Rather, let me imitate the custom of the poets and ask the gods and goddesses to give success to my words and my work.

The Story of Aeneas

Everyone generally agrees that when Troy was captured, the Greeks spared only two men: Aeneas and Antenor. This was either because they were respecting the ancient law of hospitality or because these two had always desired to return Helen and make peace. Antenor and Aeneas went in separate directions. Antenor became the leader of some Enetian exiles who had been expelled from Paphlagonia[59] in a rebellion and lost their king in the Trojan War. He led them against the Euganei, who lived in northern Italy between the Alps and the Adriatic. After defeating the Euganei, Antenor occupied their lands and named the place Troy, after his homeland. The people were called Venetians.[60]

Aeneas also fled from his homeland, but fate led him on to greater things. First, he landed in Macedonia; then he sought a home in Sicily. After leaving Sicily, he went to Laurentum, which now also bears the name of Troy. Here, the Trojans disembarked, but as they had lost almost all their things in their wanderings except their weapons and ships, they began attacking the surrounding fields. The native Latins and their king (whose name was Latinus) hurried to defend their lands.

There are two different versions of what happened next. According to one, King Latinus was defeated and made peace with Aeneas. According to the other, Latinus asked for a parley just before the two armies clashed in battle.

"Who are you men?" he asked. "What fortune compels you to leave your homes and come to these shores?"

---

[59] A region in modern day Turkey.

[60] The story of Aeneas is almost certainly the stuff of legend, but the city of Troy did exist, and it was destroyed sometime during the 13th century BC. Thus, the story of Aeneas refers to approximately that time period.

Aeneas replied, "We are Trojans, and I am Aeneas, son of Anchises and the goddess Venus. Our homeland lies in ruins, burnt to the ground by the Greeks. We come here seeking a new home."

Because Latinus admired the Trojans' nobility and saw that they were ready for both peace and war, he offered his right hand as a sign of faith and future friendship. The two leaders made a treaty, and the armies exchanged greetings. Latinus welcomed Aeneas as a guest, and Aeneas confirmed the treaty by marrying Latinus' daughter Lavinia in the sight of their tutelary gods (*penates*).[61]

The Trojans thus ended their wanderings and found a place to live. They built a city, which Aeneas called Lavinium after his wife. Shortly thereafter, Lavinia gave birth to a baby boy, whom his parents named Ascanius.

Now, Lavinia had already been promised to the King of the Rutuli, who could not bear the thought that a newcomer had been preferred to himself, so he made war on both Aeneas and the Latins. This war was tragic for both sides because the Rutuli were conquered, and the Latins lost their king.

The Rutuli then sought the aid of the Etruscan King Mezentius, who had watched the rise of the Trojans uneasily and thus welcomed a military alliance with the Rutuli. Faced with such an enemy, Aeneas took steps to win over the Latins. In order to bind the two peoples together in both law and name, Aeneas ordered the Trojans to begin calling themselves Latins. From that time on, the Latins were as faithfully devoted to Aeneas as the Trojans were.

Though the Etruscans had a reputation as a powerful nation, Aeneas did not hide behind his city walls; rather, he led his army into the open field and staked his fortune on the combined power of the Trojans and Latins, who were quickly becoming one nation. The Latins did win the battle, but Aeneas was killed. His tomb sits on the banks of the River Numicus, and rightly or wrongly, he is now called Aeneas Jupiter, Friend of the Needy.

---

[61] The *penates* were the gods who watched over individual households.

At this time, Aeneas's son Ascanius was not yet old enough to exercise *imperium*;[62] nevertheless, his mother Lavinia was a powerful woman, and she kept the ancestral throne safe for her son. The records are a little unclear on one point: we do not know whether the Julian house takes its name from this Ascanius [Iulus][63] or from an older son of Aeneas who was born in Troy and was a companion in his father's flight.[64] In any case, Ascanius was certainly the son of Aeneas.

In the following years, the city of Lavinium grew wealthy and powerful. After thirty years, Ascanius gave the city to his mother (or his stepmother) and built a new city, which was called Alba Longa because it stretched alongside the Alban hills. The defeat of the Etruscans had so increased the Latins' power that no one dared to fight them, even during the regency of a woman. The Etruscans and Latins thus had peace, and they marked their border at the river Albula, which is now called the Tiber.

Romulus and Remus

After some years, the throne descended to Numitor, who had many sons. However, his younger brother Amulius decided that force counted for more than their father's will or respect for his brother's seniority. He defeated Numitor and took the throne for himself. He then heaped crime upon crime, killing off his nephews

---

[62] The Latin word *imperium* refers to the formal power to command. It can refer to political and military power given to individuals or to the power of one nation over another. *Imperium* is the root of the modern English word "empire."

[63] The house of the Julii was an old patrician family. This is the family from which Julius Caesar was descended.

[64] Virgil adopts the latter story for the *Aeneid*; in that poem Ascanius is the son of the Trojan princess Creusa, and he accompanies his father in his wanderings.

and forcing his niece to become a Vestal Virgin,[65] so that under the pretense of honoring her, he might ensure that she could not produce any heirs.[66]

However, I think that at this point, the fates had already ordained Rome's future greatness. Even though she was a Vestal Virgin, [Numitor's daughter] Rhea Silvia was raped and gave birth to twins. She claimed the father was Mars, either because she actually believed it or because it would appear less heinous if a god was the author of the crime. Nevertheless, neither gods nor men could save her or her babies from the cruelty of the king, who imprisoned her and ordered the twins to be thrown into the river.

By chance or divine will, the Tiber had just flooded, and standing water surrounded its banks. Because it was hard to get close to the river, the king's henchmen simply left the children in the nearest pool of water, hoping the tide of the river would carry them away and drown them… but the retreating waters left the children's floating cradle on dry land, in a spot that was then a vast wilderness. Legend has it that a thirsty she-wolf that had come down from the mountains heard the crying children and ran to them. Stooping down, the she-wolf offered her teats to the crying children, who nursed at her breast. The keeper of the king's sheep, a man named Faustulus, found this gentle wolf licking the twins with her tongue and took the children to his hut for his wife Larentia to raise. Others believe that the shepherds had nicknamed Larentia "the she-wolf" because she was a whore and that it was this name that gave rise to the legend.

When the children were young boys, they worked on the farm, tended the sheep, and hunted in the woods. Blessed with strong bodies and robust spirits, they not only hunted animals but also attacked bands of thieves and stole their ill-gotten loot. They shared

---

[65] A vestal virgin was a priestess of the goddess Vesta. They took vows of celibacy.

[66] The founding of Rome by Romulus and Remus is traditionally dated to 753 BC.

their booty with the other shepherds, who formed a growing band of men engaged in both serious matters and frivolous pursuits.

Even at that time, the Festival of the Lupercalia was held on the Palatine Hill...Here an Arcadian[67] named Evander, who had settled that spot many years before, had instituted a solemn festival in which youths did homage to the god Pan,[68] running about naked for amusement and for sport. Everybody knew when the festival occurred, so some resentful thieves took the opportunity to avenge themselves by ambushing the twins during it. Romulus defended himself, but Remus was taken prisoner and handed over to King Amulius. His captors accused him of other peoples' crimes, including robbing Numitor's fields; thus, Remus was handed over to Numitor for punishment.

Now, from the beginning, Faustulus had suspected that he was bringing up the royal descendants, for he knew that the children had been exposed by the order of the king, and he knew that he had found the twins around that same time. However, he did not want to share that information too soon, so he waited for either the proper occasion or some necessity. Necessity came first. Fearing for the life of Remus, Faustulus told Romulus the truth about his birth. By chance, Numitor had heard that his prisoner had a twin brother. When he considered the boys' ages and thought about how little their characters fit their servile condition, he was reminded of his grandchildren, and he soon realized that Remus was in fact his own grandson. Thus, King Amulius was deceived by everyone.

Romulus did not attack Amulius directly, for he was no match for the king in a contest of naked force. Rather, he ordered his men

---

[67] Arcadia is a region in central Greece.

[68] Pan is the ancient Greek god of shepherds and mountain wilds. He is traditionally represented as a faun, a being with a human head and torso but goat-like legs. Arcadia was the traditional home of Pan, whose Roman name was Lupercus and who was often depicted as a sexual dynamo with an oversized phallus. Thus, he was the patron of the festival of the Lupercalia, in which youths ran around naked, engaging in a sort of fertility ritual.

to approach the city by various routes and converge on it at the same time, while Remus simultaneously led a body of armed men from Numitor's house. Numitor diverted the Alban army to the citadel by claiming that the enemy had entered the city and was attacking the king. Thus, they were able to surprise the king and kill him.

When Numitor saw the twins coming to congratulate him, he gathered an assembly of the people, told them of his brother's treachery, and recounted the story of his grandchildren, including their birth, their upbringing, and how he had recognized them. Finally, he admitted to being the author of the tyrant's destruction. The youths paraded through the ranks and saluted their grandfather; then the people elected Numitor king and gave him the *imperium*.

Romulus and Remus then wanted to build a city at the place where they had been exposed and raised. There were many Albans, Latins, and shepherds who needed a home; thus, the brothers hoped that their new city might grow so large that it would make Alba and Lavinium seem small. However, these pleasant dreams were interrupted by the ancestral curse, the lust for rule (*cupido regni*), and before long, a shameful dispute ruined this peaceful beginning.

The twins did not know who was older, so in order to decide who should rule the new city and after whom it should be named, they read the auguries of the local gods.[69] For this purpose, Romulus built a temple on the Palatine Hill, and Remus built one on the Aventine. Remus received the first augury: the appearance of six vultures. Just as this news was brought to Romulus, twelve vultures appeared to him.

Each side claimed victory. The supporters of Remus argued that his augury had appeared first; the supporters of Romulus argued that he had seen more birds. The dispute grew so heated that Remus was struck and killed. The more common story is that Remus

---

[69] The Romans believed that the will of the gods could be interpreted by reading the omens: normally either the flight paths of birds or the entrails of an animal. A modern equivalent might be Tarot cards or palm reading.

jumped over Romulus's newly built walls in order to mock his brother, and the infuriated Romulus killed him, chiding him with the words, "Let the same be done to whomever tries to take my walls." Either way, Romulus alone received the *imperium*, and the city was named after him.

Romulus first fortified the Palatine Hill, the spot where he had been raised. He established religious rites to the sacred Alban gods and adopted the rites of the Greek Hercules, which had been instituted by Evander...

Having given due respect to the divine rites, he called the multitude to an assembly and gave them laws, thinking that this was the only way to bind them together as one people. He thought that these uncivilized men would only respect the laws if he adopted the trappings of rule (*imperium*), so he surrounded himself with symbols of his authority, the most important of which were the twelve lictors.[70] Some think he chose twelve because of the number of birds that had portended his rule, but I think he adopted the custom from the Etruscans, for when the Etruscans made a king, each of the twelve Etruscan nations would give him one lictor.

Meanwhile, the city continued to expand, and Romulus extended the walls in all directions, thereby hoping to populate the city. It was an old custom in growing cities to gather together some lowly-born people and then to claim that they were born from the earth itself. Romulus granted political asylum and accepted both slaves and free men from the surrounding areas, many of whom had fled from their own homelands, eager for a fresh start; this was the first source of Rome's strength.

When he was satisfied that there were enough people, he organized a senate. He created a hundred senators, either because this number was enough or because there were only one-hundred

---

[70] The lictors originally functioned as the king's bodyguard. They had the authority to carry the *fasces*, a bundle of sticks with an axe sticking out, as a symbol of the *imperium*, or authority to rule. Later, lictors were assigned to all the Roman magistrates who held *imperium*.

suitable men for the job. They were given the title of *patres*,[71] and their children were called patricians.

The Rape of the Sabines

By this point, the Roman military was the equal of its neighbors; but Rome had no women and thus no children, so the Romans feared their power would not last. On the advice of the senate, Romulus sent embassies to the neighboring peoples, requesting alliances and wives.[72]

"Cities," the ambassadors said, "are born from humble beginnings, but with the help of the gods, cities of virtuous men grow powerful and famous. Rome lacks neither virtuous men nor the aid of the gods; thus, mixing with Romans will not corrupt your bloodlines."

Not a single city responded favorably to these entreaties since they all despised the Romans and feared Rome's growing power. Rather, the neighboring cities responded, "Why don't you grant asylum to female criminals too? That is the only way you are getting equal marriage terms with anyone."

The Roman youths could not bear this insult and thus prepared for war. Romulus, however, concealed his bitterness and prepared the solemn games in honor of Equestrian Neptune, thinking this the perfect opportunity to secure wives for the Romans. He announced to the neighboring cities that Rome would hold a great spectacle. For their part, the Romans made lavish preparations for it, hoping to draw a large crowd.

Many peoples came to these games, eager to see the new city. Foremost among these were the Caeninenses, Crustomini, and

---

[71] Literally, fathers.

[72] This story is traditionally called the Rape of the Sabines, but the reader should note that the Latin term from which it is derived, *raptus*, means abduction, not rape. There really is no perfect Latin equivalent for our word rape.

Antemnates.[73] Many Sabines came as well, bringing their wives and children. The Romans invited their guests into their homes and showed them great hospitality; the guests observed the fortifications and houses of the city, marveling at how quickly Rome had grown. Finally came the time for the show. While all eyes were on this spectacle, the signal was given, and the Roman youths proceeded to seize all the virgins in the crowd and drag them off to their houses.

Most of them were carried off willy-nilly; however, some of the patricians had selected certain of the choicest beauties ahead of time and deputed their plebeian clients to carry them off to their homes. One particularly gorgeous woman was carried off by the Thalassi family. People kept asking where they were taking her, and in order to avoid being robbed of their quarry, the plebs carried her away crying out "*thalassio.*" This is why *thalassio* is said at weddings.

Overcome by fear, the virgins' families ran away, condemning the outrage as a violation of hospitality and calling on Neptune to avenge the indignity. Nor did the virgins themselves feel any less despair and indignation.

But Romulus himself went around to all the women and said, "We have only taken you because of the pride of your fathers, who have withheld from us the right of marriage. Let go of your anger, Sabine daughters, for you are to become Roman wives and share in the fortunes of this great city. What's more? You will become the mothers of free men. So give your souls over to the destiny that fate has given your bodies. Indeed, outrage (*iniuria*) often blossoms into affection,[74] and these men will treat you better than wives, for they will be as fathers and brothers to you as well."

The men added flatteries of their own, trying to excuse the deed with protestations of passion and love, which is the best way to persuade women of anything.

---

[73] Groups from nearby cities.

[74] *Iniuria* can mean injury, outrage, or what we might call sexual assault.

Thus, the women relented of their anger, but their relatives put on mourning garb and stirred up the neighboring cities with tears and laments. Nor was their anger limited to their own cities; rather, they sent diplomats to Titus Tatius, King of the Sabines and the most powerful man in those regions. However, the Caeninenses, Crustomini, and Antemnates complained that Tatius and the Sabines acted too slowly, so these three peoples prepared to go to war by themselves. Yet the Caeninenses thought that both the Crustomini and Antemnates were too slow, so they attacked the Roman lands alone. When they were pillaging different parts of the Roman fields, Romulus attacked them with his army and defeated them easily, thus teaching them that anger is useless without numbers. He routed and pursued their army, killed the king in combat, and stripped him of his armor. Having killed the enemy leader, he took the city of Caenina on the first assault. When he returned to Rome with his victorious army, he wanted to show his military prowess to everyone, so he ascended the Capitoline[75] with the enemy king's armor hung from a litter. He hung the armor on a sacred oak and designated that spot as a temple to Jupiter, renaming him Jupiter Feretri.

He then spoke these words. "I, the victor King Romulus, bring these royal arms to you, and I dedicate a temple in this place. My descendants will bring the spoils of enemy kings to this spot."

This is the origin of the first temple consecrated in Rome. The gods assured that Romulus' descendants would fulfill his oath, but none of Rome's future success would diminish Romulus' first glory. After so many years and so many wars, these spoils have only been offered two times, so rarely does fortune consider such a prize to be fitting.

While the Romans were busy with the Caeninenses, the Antemnates army took the opportunity to attack. Romulus quickly marched the Roman legion into battle and crushed the Antemnates when they were scattered in the fields. As soon as the Roman legion

---

[75] One of the seven hills of Rome.

gave out a war cry and charged, the enemy was routed and their city captured.

While the Romans were rejoicing in their double victory, Romulus' wife Hersilia, having been worn down by the virgins' pleas, asked her husband to allow their relatives to come to the city to sue for peace. Romulus immediately granted her request, then, he made war against the Crustomini, who were much less enthusiastic after seeing the defeat of their neighbors. The Romans built colonies in the lands of the Crustomini and Antemnates, and many Romans emigrated there because of the fertility of the soil. Conversely, many of the abducted virgins' relatives immigrated to Rome from the surrounding areas.

The Sabines proved to be the most dangerous enemy, for they let neither anger nor greed dictate their tactics, nor did they reveal their military preparations until they were ready to move. To this strategy was added a little deceit. A man named Spurius Tarpeius was in charge of the Roman citadel.[76] When his daughter had gone outside the walls to fetch water for some religious ceremonies, Tatius bribed her to let his army into the citadel. Once they had captured the citadel, they killed the girl, either to make it seem as if the citadel had been taken by force or to show that promises were not to be kept with traitors. According to another story, the girl had asked to be paid with everything the Sabines wore on their left arms, the arms with which the Sabines carried their shields. Now, at that time, the Sabines were in the habit of adorning their shield arms with golden bracelets and rings, but instead of giving her these, they crushed her with the shields they carried in those arms instead. Some say that in asking for what was on their left arms, she meant their weapons and that she was going to betray them, but having seen through the fraud, the Sabines paid her back with death instead.

In any case, the Sabines now held the citadel. The next day, the Roman army drew up ranks between the Palatine and Capitoline hills, but the Sabines did not come down from the high ground until

---

[76] A citadel is a fortress that protects a town.

the infuriated Romans rushed the citadel. As the armies closed, the Sabine Mettius Curius and the Roman Hostius Hostilius flew in front of the ranks and met each other in single combat. Even though Hostilius was fighting on bad ground, his courage and audacity sustained the Roman cause, but when he was killed, the Romans immediately began to falter.

When the fleeing ranks had reached the old gate of the Palatine, Romulus threw up his arms and invoking heaven, exclaimed, "Jupiter, at the founding of this city, you sent me an augury at this spot. The Sabines have treacherously seized the citadel and having defeated us in battle, they rush into the valley. Father of gods and men, do not let our enemies pass this spot; banish fear from Roman hearts and put a stop to this flight. I vow to build a temple to you at this spot so that future generations might remember what happened here."

Having cried this out in a loud voice, he acted as if his prayers had been heard and added, "At this place, Romans, Jupiter orders you to stand your ground and fight."

The Romans fought as if the command had come from heaven itself. Romulus himself dashed forward to the front of the ranks. Now, Mettius had run out from the citadel, leading the Sabine ranks, scattering the Roman legion, and driving the Romans to the spot where the forum is now. He was nearly at the gates of the Palatine, crying, "We have conquered these treacherous weaklings; now they know how much harder it is to fight against real men than to carry off defenseless girls."

When he was thus exulting in his victory, Romulus and a band of the most ferocious young Romans set on him. Mettius was at a disadvantage because he was fighting on horseback, and the Romans easily pushed him back. Inspired by the boldness of the king, the Romans beat back the Sabines, pursued them into the valley, and routed their armies. With his horse trembling from the noise of battle, Mettius accidentally rode into a marsh. This distracted the Sabines, who went over to call out encouragement to him. He courageously extracted himself, and the Romans and the Sabines reengaged in battle in the valley, but the Romans now had the upper hand.

At this point, the Sabine virgins, who had been the original cause of the troubles, dared to fling themselves into the midst of the battle and the flying spears. Having conquered their womanly fear, they rent their garments and tore at their hair, and tried to separate the two sides, begging both to let go of their anger.

"Fathers," they pleaded, "do not shed the blood of our husbands. For you will be murdering your own sons-in-law. Husbands, our fathers are now your fathers as well. Do not stain yourselves and your children with the crime of parricide. If you cannot bear this kinship and our marriage, turn your anger on us. We are the cause of this war. We are responsible for the slaughter of our husbands and our relatives. Better that we should die than live as widows and orphans."

This appeal moved both the leaders and the multitude, and everyone fell silent. The leaders proceeded to make a treaty, agreeing to bind the two cities into one. They would share the kingship and confer all *imperium* on the Romans. The city was thus doubled, and the Romans citizens were given the name of Quirites, after the Sabine capital, Cures. They erected a monument to the battle in the place in which Mettius Curtius got his horse out of the marsh and renamed the lake after him.

Thus, misery was changed to happiness, and this episode made the Sabine women more beloved by their husbands and fathers, and most of all by Romulus himself. Thus, when he divided the people into thirty tribes, he gave one Sabine woman's name to each tribe. There were certainly more than thirty women, yet we don't know why he chose these thirty. At the same time, he conscripted three companies of knights; the Ramnenses were named after Romulus and the Titienses after Tatius; the origin of the name of the Luceres is unknown. From that point on, the kingdom was jointly and harmoniously ruled by the two kings.

The Death of Romulus

Given Romulus' accomplishments in peace and war, it seems entirely possible that he might, indeed, have been the son of a god and risen to heaven after his death, for his management of affairs secured nearly forty years of peace and safety for Rome after his death...

One day, Romulus was conducting a review of the army in the Campus Martius. All of a sudden, a loud storm arose, and Romulus was covered by a thick, dense cloud, so that no one in the assembly could see him. When the sun reappeared and had begun to calm the Romans' fears, they saw that the throne was empty. The senators who had been sitting next to him claimed that he had been taken away (*raptum*) by the whirlwind, and though the people believed the senators' story, they remained gloomily silent, so terrified were they of their loss.

Shortly thereafter, the crowd proclaimed Romulus to be a god, son of a god, king and father of the Roman city, and savior of the world, and they prayed for his help. I believe that some historians tacitly imply that the senators killed him and tore him limb-from-limb, for inklings of this tradition remained for some time. Most people, however, believed that he ascended to heaven, no doubt strengthened in their belief by their admiration for the man.

Shortly after these events, one clever Roman named Proculus Julius, a man with enough gravitas to carry authority with the assembly, lent credence to this story. Aware of the city's deep anxiety over the loss of Romulus and their anger with the senators, Julius claimed, "At the break of day, our father Romulus descended from heaven and allowed me to see him. I stood before him, rapt in terror, begging that I be absolved for looking upon him, when he said, 'Go, tell the Romans that it is heaven's will that my Rome be head of all the world. Thus, look to your military, and let your descendants know that no human efforts will be able to resist the Romans. Having spoken these lofty words, he left." It is amazing how much the Romans trusted this man's story, and once they were convinced of the immortality of Romulus, they were much less afraid.

The Horatii

*Livy then recounts that after the death of Romulus, the Romans elected
Numa Pompilius as their king, who was distinguished for his piety and
introduced many religious customs in Rome. We pick back up with Livy's
history with the election of Rome's third king, Tullus Hostilius and the story
of the Horatii.*

When Numa died, the republic passed into an interregnum.[77]
Tullus Hostilius, the grandson of that Hostilius who had famously
fought the Sabines in front of the citadel, was elected king by the
people and confirmed by the senate. Tullus was not peace-loving like
Numa; rather, he was even fiercer than Romulus. He was young and
hungry for glory, and he was convinced that the city's idleness was
making it weak, so he tried to start a war; any sort of war would do.

It happened that the Romans had plundered some of the Alban
fields, and the Albans had in turn plundered some of the Roman
fields. Both sides simultaneously sent diplomats to the other,
demanding restitution. Tullus had ordered his diplomats to make
their demands immediately because he was sure that the Albans
would reject them, and then he would have a legitimate excuse for
war. For his part, he prevented the Alban legates from immediately
making their demands by receiving them cordially and idling away
the time in feasting. Meanwhile, the Romans demanded restitution
from the Albans. When the Albans rejected their demands, the
Romans declared that war would begin in thirty days. They sent the
message to Tullus, who then allowed the Alban diplomats to speak.

The diplomats did not know that war had already been
declared, so they said, "We do not intend to say anything displeasing
to you, but our superiors compel us to demand the return of our
goods. We are ordered to say that if they are not returned, we will
declare war."

Tullus responded, "Tell your king that I call upon the gods to
bring ruin on whichever one of us is the first to reject the others'

---

[77] An interregnum is a period between reigns when there is no king.

diplomats." This news was brought to Alba, and both sides prepared for war.

This war was almost like a civil war between parents and children since both sides were descendants of the Trojans. The Trojans had settled Lavinium. Lavinium had colonized Alba, and Alba had given birth to the Roman kings. This, however, made the war less brutal, for there were no pitched battles, and when the roofs of one side were pulled down, the two people became one.

First, the vast Alban army attacked the Roman fields. They pitched camp about five miles from the city, in a place surrounded by a ditch; for some time after, the ditch was called the *Fossa Cluilia* after the Alban leader, Gaius Cluilius, until time destroyed both the ditch and the name. During the war, Cluilius died in camp, and the Albans made Mettius Fufetius dictator. Meanwhile, Tullus grew even fiercer, saying the gods had killed Cluilius as a warning: soon they would punish the rest of the Albans with the same fate.

Bypassing the enemy camp at night, the Roman army entered Alban territory. This roused Mettius. He led his army as near to the enemy as possible and requested a parley, saying that Tullus could be sure that what he had to say would be no less useful to the Romans than to the Albans. Tullus accepted the proposal, but he drew his army into ranks just in case the talks came to nothing.

After both sides had instructed their men to stay in place, the leaders and a few noblemen advanced into the middle.

Then Mettius said, "I seem to have heard our king say that we are fighting this war over some stolen property. Doubtless, you claim the same thing, Tullus. But the truth of the matter is that this war is really a contest for empire. I will not second-guess my king's decision, but now I am the leader of the Albans, and I want to give you a warning, Tullus: we are surrounded on all sides by the mighty Etruscans. Remember, when you give the sign to start the fight, the Etruscans will be watching this spectacle, and after we have weakened each other, they will attack us both. If we are not content with certain liberty, if we must roll the dice and risk slavery to win empire, by all means, let us do it. But, for god's sake, let's avoid ruin and bloodshed."

Even though he was a much fiercer man and had more hope of victory, Tullus agreed, and fortune itself soon provided the method. It happened by chance that both armies contained sets of triplets who were similar in both age and strength. We know that they were called the Horatii and Curiatii, though we don't know which brothers were Roman and which brothers were Alban, even though this is the most famous story from all antiquity. Many historians say that the Horatii were Romans, so we will go with the majority opinion.

The kings made a treaty agreeing that the triplets would battle to the death in a sword fight and the winning side would be granted *imperium*...

Having made this treaty, the two ferocious sets of triplets seized their weapons and entered the space between the armies, with the exhortations of their respective sides ringing in their ears. Both sides exhorted their champions to remember that their countrymen, their kinsmen, and the gods of their fathers were watching their actions. Both sides watched the battle in front of their camps, freed from present danger but not from the fear in their hearts, for the fates of their respective empires hung in the balance.

The sign was given, and the youths ran at each other like two little armies, carrying the burdens of the larger armies in their souls. Neither side paid any attention to the danger, for their only thought was to win an empire for their country and avoid delivering it into slavery: everything depended on them.

At the first clash, their arms rattled and their swords gleamed, and the spectators were overwhelmed with awe. Neither side immediately gained the upper hand, and the crowd soon quieted as their spirits sank. Bodies clashed, spears flew, and at last blood was drawn; two Romans had fallen dead, one on top of the other. All three Albans were wounded. The Albans shouted for joy; the Romans sunk in despair, dismayed by the new odds.

Fortunately, the last Roman was unharmed. He knew that he could not fight all three of his opponents simultaneously, but he thought he could beat them one at a time. Thus, he fled from the spot, thinking that each of his opponents would chase him as their various wounds would allow and arrive at him one by one. Having run some distance, he turned and saw that there was a gap between each of his pursuers, so he reentered the fray, and killed the first attacker, amidst the shouts of the Alban army exhorting the straggling Curiatii to come to their brother's aid. Then, Horatius closed with the second. Seeing this unexpected turn of events, the Romans lifted the spirits of their champion with their war cry; and he hurried to finish the fight. The third brother was not far off, but Horatius killed his adversary before the third brother could arrive. The untouched Horatius drew strength from his two victories; the third Curiatii practically gave up in despair, for he was wounded and tired, and the sight of his brothers' dead body took all the fight out of him. In a moment, Horatius had him on the ground.

Exalting over his defeated opponent, Horatius crowed, "I dedicated the first two for my slain brothers, this third I consecrate to the cause of this fight: that Romans might rule over Albans."

He then struck his sword into the throat of his opponent, who could barely lift his own shield to defend himself. Then Horatius stripped his enemy's weapons and armor.

All the Romans' fear turned to joy, as they cheered and congratulated the surviving brother. The two sides then turned their attention to burying their champions, though with very different spirits, for the one side had enlarged its empire, and the other side was given over to a foreign power. The graves still stand at the place where the men fell, the two Romans closer to Alba and the three Albans at some distance towards Rome.

Before the armies dispersed, Mettius asked Tullus for his commands. Tullus ordered the Albans to remain in arms, which they would need if there was a war with the Veientes.[78] Then, both armies returned to their homes. Horatius led the army home, carrying the arms of the triplets he had killed.

---

[78] A neighboring city.

Now, Horatius had one sister, who had been betrothed to one of the Curiatii. She was awaiting the army's return in front of the Capena Gate, and recognizing that the cloak her brother was carrying over his shoulder belonged to her betrothed (for she had made it with her own hands), she tore at her hair and tearfully cried out the dead man's name. This infuriated the fierce young Horatii, who pulled out his sword and ran the girl through, angrily exclaiming, "Since you have forsaken your brother and your fatherland, go to live with your beloved husband among the dead. So let it be done to any Roman who mourns for the enemy."

Everyone considered this a savage crime, though somewhat excusable given the young man's recent accomplishments. Nevertheless, he was taken to be judged by the king. Tullus did not want the common people to think him ungrateful by condemning and executing this man, so he convoked an assembly and appointed two men to judge the case. If Horatius were found guilty, he was to be whipped and then taken outside the walls to be hung from a tree. The judges did not think they had the right to absolve even harmless persons, so they proclaimed Horatius guilty of treason, condemned him to punishment, and told the lictor to bind his hands.

While the lictor was binding the noose, Horatius appealed the verdict to the Assembly of the People.[79] His father spoke on his behalf with these words, "Men of the Assembly. Do not condemn my son to death, for my daughter has been justly slain. Indeed, were her death not just, I would have taken the right of a father and executed the boy myself. Consider my fate, men of Rome. Just a short time ago, I was the father of a large family. Now, you are about to take away my last child."

Then the father tearfully embraced his son and pointed to the spoils that his son had taken from the Curiatii, which were fixed on the place that is now called the Pila Horatia. "Roman citizens," he pleaded, "look at the man whom you have just cheered in victory. Can you bear to see him bound, whipped, and tortured? Can you

---

[79] The legislative body that consisted of all Roman citizens.

bear to see him hanging from the gallows? Even Alban eyes could hardly bring themselves to look upon such a shameful spectacle. Go then, lictor. Bind the hands that have just won an empire for the Roman people. Cover the head that has just liberated the city. Whip his body in the city—in plain sight of the spoils of his enemy. Or if you cannot, whip him outside of the city, amongst the graves of the Curiatii. Where can you take this youth where his glories will not vindicate so disgraceful a punishment?"

The people could not bear the father's tears or bring themselves to execute so courageous a youth, so they let him go, though it was more in admiration of his virtues than because of the justness of his case. In order to expiate such a manifest murder with some little offering, the father was ordered to make some expiation for his son at the public expense. Having made a few little sacrifices, he put up a beam over the street, and made his son walk under it with his head covered as if in a yoke. Today, this beam, which is known as the sister's beam, is kept up at the public expense. They built a stone grave for the sister at the spot where she died.

Tarquin the Proud

After the story of the Horatii, Livy recounts the reigns of the next three kings of Rome: Ancus Marcius, Priscus Tarquin, and Servius Tullius. According to Livy, Servius was the child of a captured Latin princess and was given in marriage to a daughter of the Roman king, Priscus Tarquin. When the king died, Servius' mother-in-law engineered his election as king by the senate (without the involvement of the Roman people).

Livy describes Servius as a wise king who ruled for more than four decades, extended the franchise to the plebs, and instituted the census. Nevertheless, Servius faced the hostile ambitions of his predecessor's son: Lucius Tarquin, later known as Tarquin the Proud. [80]

---

[80] Tarquin the Proud ruled from 535 BC to 509 BC, the latter of which is the date that is traditionally given for the establishment of the Roman republic.

Although Servius had been the undisputed ruler for some time, he had heard that Lucius Tarquin was complaining that he did not rule by the consent of the people, so Servius secured his popularity with the plebs by dividing some seized lands amongst them. Then he dared to ask the people whether or not they commanded him to reign, and he was proclaimed king with as much support as any previous king had ever had.

Yet this did not diminish Tarquin's hope of becoming king, rather he desired it all the more, for he sensed that the patricians were unhappy about the distribution of land, so he took every opportunity to criticize Servius in front of the patricians and increase his influence in the senate. In all of this, he was inflamed by the restless spirit of youth and prodded by his wife Tullia, who was herself a restless woman.

Indeed, his wicked seizure of power would make for a good tragic play, yet because of it, the Romans tired of kingship and won a more complete liberty, for Tarquin's reign would be the last that might arise from such evil.

This Lucius Tarquin was either the grandson or, more likely, the son of King Priscus Tarquin.[81] He had a brother named Arruns, who was a gentle youth. He and his brother were married to Servius' daughters, both of whom also had very different characters. Fortune had given the wicked sister to Arruns, thereby preventing the vicious pair from joining in matrimony until the Roman people had grown accustomed to the changes Servius had made to the constitution. At least, that is what I believe.

The wicked daughter, Tullia, was annoyed that her husband neither acted boldly nor lusted for power, so she turned all her attentions on Lucius, whom she admired as a man worthy of his royal blood. Tullia despised her sister because though she had got herself a real man for a husband, she lacked the boldness to be a real woman.

---

[81] Actually, simple math would suggest that it is more likely that he was Priscus Tarquin's grandson.

Lucius Tarquin and Tullia thus found themselves drawn together by their common natures: Tullia made Lucius ready for any wickedness, but she alone was the cause of all the troubles.

She used to meet Lucius in secret and criticize their respective spouses. "Wouldn't it be better," she mused, "for me to be a widow and you a widower than to remain tied down to these lazy spouses and thereby lose our own youthful vigor? If the gods had given me a real man for a husband, I would see to it that he would soon wield my father's power."

In this way, she filled the young man with her own boldness, and they soon conspired to kill their respective spouses and marry each other. Servius did not exactly approve of this union, but he did not explicitly forbid it either.

Thus, Servius found himself beset by problems in his old age, as his daughter flitted from one crime to the next. At each step she egged her husband on, spurring him to the next crime by arguing that if they did not carry it through, their previous crimes would have been in vain.

"I was not looking for a mere husband or a partner in servitude," she claimed, "I need a man who thinks himself worthy of a kingdom. Who remembers that he is the son of Priscus Tarquin and who wants to actually have a throne, not just dream about it."

"If you are the man I think I married, I shall call you both husband and king. If you are less than that, I made a poor trade, for my current husband is a criminal as well as a coward. What will you do, then? You are not from Corinth, nor from Tarquin like your father. You do not need to struggle for a foreign kingdom. The Tarquin name makes you king. Your ancestral gods proclaim it. The image of your father impressed upon your face affirms it. Will you disappoint your city? Why do you allow the young nobles to consider you their king, if you are not going to do anything about it? Return, in that case, to Tarquin or Corinth and to the house of your ancestors, for you are a coward like your brother, not a king like your father."

Chiding him with complaints like this, she incited Tarquin to wicked deeds, for she herself was greedy for power.

Roused by his wife's womanly frenzies, Tarquin went around to various senators, mainly those of the lesser houses. He reminded them of the benefits his father had bestowed on them and asked for their favor in return, binding the youths to him with gifts. Thus, he mainly increased his support by bribing senators and criticizing the king.

At last, seeing that the time for action was at hand, he came into the forum with a body of armed men. As everyone was shaking with fear, he sat on the royal throne in front of the senate house and announced that the senators were to gather in the presence of King Tarquin. A group quickly assembled, some of whom had been prepared for the coup beforehand, others who feared harm if they did not come, thinking that Servius' power would soon be at an end.

Tarquin began by criticizing Servius. "Your so-called king," he proclaimed, "is a slave who was born of slaves. He received the throne as a gift from his wife after the disgraceful death of his father-in-law. He did not observe the customary interregnum and has neither been elected by the assembly nor by the people, nor has he been confirmed by the authority of the senate.[82] This slave has won his throne illegally, and held onto it by exploiting the divisions of the patricians and by bribing the mob. He has placed all the republic's burdens on the backs of the wealthy, burdens that heretofore have been jointly born by all of the republic. The census that he has instituted is a sham, meant to stir up the resentment of the poor against the wealthy, whose fortunes he will one day give over to the rabble to secure his power."

When a breathless messenger finally got word to Servius, he immediately went to the entrance of the senate and called out in a loud voice, "What are you doing here, Tarquin? With what audacity have you dared to assemble the senate and sit on my throne while I still live?"

---

[82] Tarquin's claim here is dubious.

Tarquin responded fiercely, "I am sitting on the throne of my father, for the son of a king is a much fitter ruler than the child of slaves, and I have tolerated your fraud long enough."

A great clamor arose from supporters of both sides, and a mass of people rushed to the senate, as it was now clear that whoever won this fight would win the throne. For Tarquin, there was no going back.

The younger and stronger Tarquin seized Servius around the waist, dragged him out of the senate house, and threw him down the steps; then he went back into the senate to bring the senators to obedience. The king's companions fled, and without his royal escort, the wounded Servius was caught and killed by Tarquin's henchmen. It is believed that this was done on the advice of Tullia, for this wickedness would be entirely in keeping with her character.

It is also agreed that Tullia rode a chariot to the forum, ignored the assembly of patricians who were there, called her husband out of the senate house, and was the first to salute him as king. Tarquin ordered her to get off the streets, so she departed by chariot. When she came to the top of Cyprus Street, where the temple of Diana used to stand, and the chariot was turning right to go up the Esquiline Hill, her terrified charioteer stopped the horses abruptly and pointed to the dead body of Servius lying in the street.

Tradition has it that the ghosts of her murdered relatives stirred Tullia into a frenzy. "Drive over it," she ordered, and her driver did, splattering blood all over the chariot and on Tullia herself, who shamelessly carried it back to her house and to her household gods. The anger of these gods, however, would one day avenge her crimes. The spot where this outrage occurred is now called the Street of the Crime.

Servius Tullius had reigned forty-four years, and even a wise and moderate successor would have had a hard time bettering him. Indeed, Servius carries a particular glory in Roman history as the last just and legitimate king. Though he exercised a moderate and mild *imperium*, some authorities claim he planned to lay his power down completely because he did not approve of monarchy in principle, but

Tarquin committed his wicked insurrection before Servius could do so.

Lucius Tarquin thus began his reign. He was called Tarquin the Proud, a nickname which he surely deserved. He began his reign by forbidding Servius burial, pointing out that Romulus, the father of all Romans, had not been buried.[83] He killed all of Servius' supporters and surrounded himself with an armed guard, so as to prevent anyone from taking the throne from himself in the same way he had taken it from Servius. Neither the people nor the senate ever elected him, and therefore having no right to rule, he ruled by force. Since he could not hope to safeguard his reign by winning the city's love (*caritas*), he ruled by fear. To inspire fear, he judged capital crimes by himself and used this power to kill and exile his opponents and seize the goods of both enemies and neutral parties alike.

He greatly diminished the number of senators, thinking a smaller senate would be less esteemed and less able to restrict his own power. He was the first king in Roman history who did not consult the senate on important matters; rather, he only asked advice from his own circle of advisors. He made war, peace, treaties, and alliances by himself and with whomever he wanted, never on the orders of the people or the senate. He made friends and marriage alliances with the other Latin peoples so that they might protect him from his own citizens. He gave his daughter to Octavius Mamilius of Tusculum, who was from a well respected Latin family that was allegedly descended from Ulysses and Circe.[84] By this marriage, Tarquin won over many of Mamilius' relatives and friends.

---

[83] According to Livy, the people of Rome believed that Romulus had ascended into heaven on a whirlwind; thus, he had not had a burial. Livy means his audience to understand that Tarquin was making a particularly tasteless joke here.

[84] Ulysses was the semi-legendary Greek hero, whose wanderings after the Trojan War are recounted by Homer in the Odyssey. Circe was a demi-goddess who enchanted Ulysses' crew.

Tarquin held great authority among the Latin nobles, so one day he ordered them to an assembly at the Grove of Ferentina, telling them that he wanted to discuss some matters of common interest. The group met at dawn on the appointed day, but Tarquin did not arrive until just before dusk. While they were waiting for Tarquin, a Latin king named Turnus criticised him in a speech.

"Little wonder that the Romans call him Tarquin the Proud, even though they only whisper it secretly. What could be more prideful than to play these games with the whole of the Latin nation? He was the one who called this meeting and asked us to travel far from our homes, yet he himself has not come. This is clearly a ruse to test our patience, so that if we accept this outrage, he might know that he can oppress us all. Do you not see that he wants to extend his *imperium* over the Latins? I won't say whether his own citizens were wise to give him *imperium*. Indeed, I will not say whether they gave it to him at all or whether he seized it by murder. In any case, the Latins should not let this foreigner have *imperium* over us. His own people are sick of him; for he kills, exiles, and robs one after another. Should we Latins expect any better treatment from this man? Listen to me. Let us go back to our homes. Let's not give this assembly any more of our time than Tarquin has."

While all these words were being uttered by a man who had himself won power in his own land through sedition and crime, Tarquin arrived. This put a stop to Turnus' speech. Everyone turned away from Turnus and saluted Tarquin. With the assembly quiet, the men standing near Tarquin asked him to explain the reason for his delay. "I apologize for my lateness," he said, "I have been mediating a dispute between father and son. We will attend to the business at hand tomorrow."

Turnus did not take this news quietly. He left the meeting with a parting shot, saying "Nothing should be quicker than settling a dispute between father and son. It can be done with a few words. Tell the son to obey his father or suffer the consequences."

Tarquin pretended to be unfazed by Turnus' remark, but he immediately began thinking about how to kill Turnus and thereby terrorize the Latins in the same way he had terrorized his own people. However, Tarquin could not put Turnus to death on his own public authority, so he destroyed his innocent opponent with false accusations, for that night, he bribed one of Turnus' slaves to let a number of swords and arms be secretly smuggled into Turnus' lodging.

The next day, Tarquin rose a little before dawn and summoned the Latin princes. Acting as if he had just discovered something disturbing, he claimed, "The gods themselves must have delayed me yesterday to keep us all safe. I have been informed that Turnus plans to kill us all and take the *imperium* for himself. He would have done it yesterday at the assembly had I arrived earlier. That is why he was so bothered by my absence; it prevented him from carrying out his plan. There is no doubt, if my informants speak the truth, that Turnus will come to the assembly today with armed men, for he has amassed a great number of swords. Let's go together to Turnus' lodgings; there, we can quickly determine whether these reports are true."

Several things made the story plausible: the plot was the sort of thing that might be expected of the ferocious Turnus, he had made that speech the previous day, and Tarquin's late arrival could account for the delay of the massacre. The Latin princes were inclined to trust Tarquin, but prepared to disbelieve him if the swords were not discovered.

Having come to the place, the guards surrounded Turnus and awoke him from his slumber. They also seized his servants, who were preparing to put up a fight. They found swords in every corner of the lodgings, which was enough to convince the Latins of Turnus' guilt. They put him in chains, called the assembly, and brought forth the evidence. The Latin princes were furious, and they condemned Turnus to death without even giving him a trial, subjecting him to a novel form of capital punishment: he was laid on a raft, weighted with stones, and then thrown headlong into the water. This punishment was carried out on the suggestion of Tarquin himself.

At the assembly, Tarquin praised the Latins, "You have done right in executing this man. Now, I want to speak of a different matter. It is in my power to exercise an ancient right. Because all the Latins come from Alba, Alba once had the power to make a federation of all the Latin peoples. However, Alba's powers were transferred to Rome under Tullus Hostilius, so this power now resides in Rome. It is in all of our interests that this alliance be renewed, for then you Latins will share in the fortunes of the Roman people rather than be afraid that we Romans will devastate your lands as we did during the reign of Ancus and my own father."

The Latins were easily persuaded by this, even though Rome was to be the preeminent state in the alliance, for the Latin princes were all in agreement with Tarquin, who had just given a fresh warning of the dangers of opposing him. In accordance with the renewal of the treaty, Latins of military age assembled at the Ferentina Grove. In order to prevent the Latins from retaining their own commanders and insignia, he mixed the Roman and Latin ranks into new legions, doubled their size, and placed a centurion in charge of each.

Though Tarquin was an unjust king, he was not a bad military commander, and his military prowess would have rivalled other kings if the same degeneracy he showed in other things had not overshadowed his military glory. He started a war with the Volscians that ended up lasting two hundred years. During this war, the Romans seized the town of Suessa Pometia. Tarquin's share of the booty came to forty silver talents,[85] and he decided to use it to build a bigger temple to Jupiter, one that might be worthy of the king of gods and men, worthy of the Roman *imperium,* and worthy of Rome itself.

His next war went more slowly than he hoped, for his opponents, the Gabii, repelled his first attempt to besiege their town,

---

[85] It is impossible to give a modern equivalent to this amount, but inasmuch as a talent was equivalent to about 70 pounds, forty talents of silver would have represented a substantial amount.

so he withdrew from the walls.   Disappointed by this defeat, he proceeded to conquer the Gabii in a most un-Roman way: by fraud and deceit. First, he pretended that he was done with the war, acting as if he was only concerned with laying the foundations of Jupiter's temple and with other works in the city.   Then, he had his youngest son Sextus pretend to defect to the Gabii, fooling them with fake complaints about his father's intolerable cruelty.

"My father," Sextus complained, "has begun to tyrannize his own family now. He is tired of his many children and freedmen, so he is preparing to kill us all just as he has killed all the senators, lest he leave behind descendants or heirs to the throne. I myself just barely slipped past the man's swords and spears. Now, I am only safe amongst you, my father's enemies."

"Do not be deceived," he continued, "his war with you is not over. He is simply waiting for you to drop your guard, so that he can invade your lands. But if a refugee like myself is not welcome here, I will go to beg at the doors of all the Latin nations until I find a people who know how to protect a child from the cruelty of his father. Perhaps, I will even find a people ready to wage war against such a tyrant."

The Gabii were worried that he would leave in anger, so they welcomed him, assuring him with conciliatory words. "Do not be amazed that your father would do such things. After committing so many crimes against the city and his allies, he has finally done the same to his family. If he ran out of victims, he would probably have to turn his blade on himself, so wild a man is he. We are grateful that you have come. With your help, our armies will be at the gates of Rome in no time."

Sextus was admitted to the public meetings, where he won favor by agreeing with the things that the older and more knowledgeable Gabii said. However, on many occasions, he said something like the following, "You ought to listen to me, Gabii. I know the strength of both yourselves and the Romans. The Roman people hate their king; indeed, even his own family hates him. It would be smart to make war on them now."

When he had thus incited the Gabii, he began going on little military expeditions into Roman territory. Everything he said and did was calculated to deceive the Gabii and increase their empty faith in him until at last, the Gabii chose him as their commander.

The multitude was completely unaware of Sextus' bad faith, and when he won a number of little skirmishes, the Gabii grew convinced that he was a gift from the gods themselves. He endured the same rigors as other soldiers and distributed the booty so generously and with such charity that he became just as powerful amongst the Gabii as his father was in Rome.

When he perceived that his men were ready to follow him anywhere and that the Gabii would agree to anything he suggested, he sent a messenger to his father for orders. Tarquin did not trust his son, so he said nothing in response to the messenger. Acting as though he were deliberating, Tarquin silently walked into his garden and struck the heads off the tallest poppies with his walking stick.

The messenger followed but soon grew weary of awaiting a response, so he returned to Sextus, reporting, "Your father did not say a word, though whether out of anger or his usual arrogance, I do not know. All he did was to walk in the garden and strike the heads of the tallest poppies with his stick."

Sextus immediately understood his father's silent commands and obeyed them by inciting the Gabii to kill some of the foremost men of their city. Many were killed by legal means; those who could not be found guilty of even trumped-up charges were killed secretly. Some were allowed to flee; others were ordered into exile. The goods of both the exiled and the executed were seized and divided amongst the people. Sextus doled out these private benefits to sweeten the bitter pill of public calamity, but once the Gabii had lost most of their foremost citizens, he betrayed them to the Roman king without any fight at all.

Having conquered the Gabii, Tarquin made peace with the Aequians and renewed the treaty with the Tuscans.[86] Then he turned

---

[86] A region to the north of Rome.

his attention to domestic affairs. The most important of these projects concerned completing the temple that his father had vowed to Jupiter, for he wanted to leave behind a monument to his reign and his name…The king's plans for the temple grew ever more elaborate, and the cost quickly became more than he could afford on his own; in fact, he could not even pay for the foundations by himself…

Nevertheless, Tarquin was intent on finishing the temple, so he summoned workers from everywhere in Tuscany. To complete the work, he used money from the public treasury and even conscripted the plebs to work on it, this in addition to their military service. This labor, however, was not as big a burden to the plebs as Tarquin's later projects: namely, constructing the seats of the circus[87] and digging out the sewer system (*cloaca maxima*). Yet, no modern work can equal either of these in scale and magnificence. After the plebs were finished with these labors, he sent them out to establish colonies, both to expand his empire and to avoid the burden of an idle multitude in the city. He sent colonists to Signia and Circeii to serve as buffer states.

Around this time, the court was terrified by the appearance of a bad omen: a snake slithering out from a wooden column at the palace. The king was not afraid of the snake, but the omen filled him with worry and anxiety. He could not use the Tuscan soothsayers (who were only summoned for public omens) to interpret his own private portent, so he sent two of his sons to journey through unknown lands to visit the famous Oracle at Delphi.[88]

Titus and Arruns undertook the journey, taking their cousin Lucius Junius Brutus as their companion. Now, Brutus was a man

---

[87] In ancient Rome, a circus was a stadium designed for chariot races. It was in the shape of a circle (actually more like an oval); hence the name circus.

[88] Delphi was a sacred site in Greece, famous for the priestess, or oracle, who supposedly channeled the god Apollo to give prophecies. The oracle, however, was famous for giving vague prophecies that were often misinterpreted by the hearers.

who was much cleverer than he let on. When he had heard that his uncle Tarquin was murdering noble Romans (even Brutus's own brother), he feigned stupidity so that the king might have nothing to fear from him. He also refrained from amassing a fortune which the king might covet. He knew that there was no safety in the laws, so he let Tarquin do whatever he wanted with his property and defended himself from his uncle by allowing others to disrespect him; he even let people call him Brutus (a name that means stupid). However, the name was like his cloak; in reality, he was simply waiting for his chance to show his courage and liberate the Roman people.

Thus, the Tarquins took him to Delphi more as their jester than as their companion. It is said that he brought a gift for Apollo, a gold staff enclosed in a wooden one, which was meant to symbolize his own character. After the brothers had carried out their father's request, they were overwhelmed by a desire to know which brother would inherit the throne. Out of the deep abyss came a voice that said the *imperium* of Rome would go to the one who kissed his mother first. As Sextus had remained at Rome, the Tarquin brothers commanded everyone to keep silent about the prophecy. As for themselves, they cast lots to decide which of them would go to Rome to kiss their mother first.

Brutus, however, thought the prophecy meant something else, and falling to the ground as if he had stumbled, he touched his lips to Mother Earth. Then they returned to Rome, which was preparing for war with the Rutuli.

The Rape of Lucretia

The Rutuli were a wealthy people who held the region of Ardea. Their wealth was the cause of the war, for Tarquin had exhausted his funds in building public works and sought to enrich himself and quell his own unpopularity by looting the Rutuli. He tried to seize the territory quickly, but when this failed, he besieged them instead.[89]

In wars such as these, which are long but not especially fierce, soldiers are granted frequent leave, especially if they are nobles. Thus, Tarquin's sons wasted much time in laziness, banquets, and merrymaking. During one of Sextus' drinking parties, a debate arose over who had the best wife. Each man praised his wife in many ways, and the dispute grew heated, whereat Sextus' cousin Collatinus claimed that he could show the superiority of his wife Lucretia in a matter of hours.

"We are young, yet," he challenged his comrades, "Let us ride home and drop in unexpectedly on our wives. What we see them doing when we are not there will show us their true characters."

They all enthusiastically agreed.

Arriving in Rome just after dark, they found most of their wives wasting their time in feasting and luxury with other nobles; Lucretia, however, was not. When they reached her house in Collatia,[90] they found her sitting amongst her ladies-in-waiting and spinning wool by lamp light. Thus, Lucretia was clearly the victor in this contest of womanly virtue.

She welcomed her husband and the other Tarquins and invited them all to dine. At dinner, both the beauty and presumed chastity of Lucretia pricked Sextus with an evil desire to defile her. He did nothing at that time, and after dinner, they returned to camp.

A few days later, Sextus showed back up at Collatinus' house. Lucretia welcomed him warmly and fed him dinner; then he was given a room in the guest quarters. After Sextus saw that all the guards were asleep, he drew his sword and snuck into the sleeping Lucretia's bedchamber.

---

[89] This story recounts an episode that we would certainly call a rape; yet, even the Latin word that Livy uses for this story, *stupra*, does not quite approximate our modern word rape, as it can refer both to forcible violation and to adultery.

[90] A city about 15 miles from Rome.

While he held her down with one hand, he pressed his blade against her with the other, threatening, "Keep your mouth shut, Lucretia. I am Sextus Tarquin. I have a blade in my hand, and if you make a sound, I will slit your throat."

The terrified Lucretia awoke to the threat of imminent death; indeed, there was no help in sight.

Tarquin confessed his love. He begged. He threatened. He pleaded. He said anything he could think of to sway a woman's heart. When he saw that not even the fear of death could move her, he threatened her with shame.

"If you do not let me have my way with you," he hissed, "I will kill you and strangle your manservant. Then I will place your nude bodies together in your bed, so it will seem that you have been justly slain in the filthy act of adultery."

This threat finally conquered Lucretia's chastity, and Tarquin took her feminine honor. After he left, the miserable Lucretia sent messengers to her father at Rome and to her husband at Ardea, telling them to come at once and bring one trusted friend, for a horrible thing had happened, and it demanded action. By chance, her husband brought Junius Brutus, who was just then returning to Rome from Delphi.

They found the unhappy woman sitting in a small room. At their arrival, she burst into tears.

"Are you well?" the men asked.

"Hardly," she responded, "for how can a defiled woman be well? Another man has stained your sheets, Collatinus. His traces still remain there. Yet though my body has been violated, my soul is yet pure. Death will be witness to my innocence. Give me your word, men; punish the man who raped me, for it was Sextus Tarquin. A few days ago he came here as my guest, but last night he came as my enemy. He has taken my happiness from me; now you must take away his. Promise me, as you are men; Sextus must pay."

As they promised this, they tried to console her. "It is not your fault. Sextus alone has committed a crime. Only the mind can sin, and a woman who does not consent cannot be at fault."

But she could not be consoled. "You men," she said, "will see to it that Sextus gets what he deserves. I absolve myself from this sin. I do not ask pardon, but no unchaste woman will ever choose to live because of my example."

With these words, she pulled out a dagger that she had hidden under her clothes and stabbed it into her heart, dying on the spot.

Her husband and father cried out in sorrow, but Brutus bent down and took the bloody dagger from Lucretia's wound. Holding it in front of himself, he vowed "With the gods as my witness, I swear by this most chaste blood that I will drive out Lucius Tarquin, together with his wicked wife and all of his wicked family. I will spare them neither sword nor fire nor anything in my power. No Tarquin, nor any man, will ever rule Rome as king again."

He then handed the blade to Collatinus. The other men were awestruck at the change that had come over Brutus, wondering where this man had come from. Brutus made them swear to avenge Lucretia, and all of their grief was thereby turned to anger. He then called them to abolish the kingship, and they followed him as their leader.

They carried Lucretia's body out of the house and into the forum, inciting the people to rebellion with news of this atrocity. Moved to tears by the sadness of Lucretia's father, the people each added their own complaints of royal wickedness

Brutus, however, chastised them. "Stop your lamenting and complaining and act like real men," he said. "Act like true Romans. Pick up your weapons and fight your enemies."

The fiercest youths immediately heeded Brutus' call, and the rest soon followed. Some of the men stood guard at the gates of Collatia to prevent anyone from bringing word of the uprising to the king; the others set out for Rome. When they arrived there, this mob of armed men threw everyone into a panic, which only died down when the people realized that the mob was composed of some of the leading men of Rome and that something important was afoot. Lucretia's rape raised just as much uproar in Rome as it had in Collatia, and people hurried to the forum from all corners of the city.

The crier then summoned them to hear the Tribune of the Celeres, which office Brutus happened to be holding at the time. Brutus delivered an oration that amazed all those who had hitherto considered him an imbecile.

"Gentlemen and plebs of Rome," he said, "the son of your king is a lustful and violent man. He has forced himself on the noble and chaste matron Lucretia. In shame, she has taken her own life. In shame, her father hangs his head in sorrow, more for the cause of her death than the death itself."

"Your king," he continued, "is a proud and arrogant man. He has set the plebs to digging ditches for his sewers. He has made you, you Romans who are the conquerors of all the surrounding nations, into workmen and stonecutters. He has most shamefully taken his throne from his father-in-law, whose dead body his wife crushed under the wheels of her chariot. Let the vengeance of the gods rain down on the Tarquins for these atrocities. Let us, Romans, be rid of kings forever. Let us be rid of Tarquin. Let us be rid of his whole stinking brood. Now is the time to live free, Romans."

Having incited the crowd, Brutus and a group of volunteers marched to the army in Ardea to incite them to insurrection. He left Lucretia's father, then serving as prefect of the city, in charge at Rome. During these tumults, Tullia fled her home and was cursed by everyone she passed, who invoked the fury of her murdered victims.

When news of the uprising reached camp, the frightened king went to Rome to put down the rebellion. Brutus heard of the king's route and changed his own, in order to avoid him on the road. Thus, Brutus reached Ardea about the same time that Tarquin reached Rome. At Rome, Tarquin found the gates closed against him and a sentence of exile passed on his person. Brutus, on the other hand, was welcomed jubilantly by the army, which expelled the king's sons from camp. Two sons followed their father into exile in Etruria. Sextus went to the Gabii, which he thought of as his own kingdom, but they killed him on account of the old feuds that his murders and thefts had stirred up.

Lucius Tarquin the Proud reigned twenty-five years. By this point, Rome had been ruled by kings for 244 years. The prefect of the city then elected Brutus and Collatinus as the first two consuls in the Assembly of the Centuries,[91] in accordance with the regulations of Servius Tullius.

The Sons of Brutus

From this point on, I shall write the history of a free Roman people, recording their deeds in peace and war, their annually elected officials, and the *imperium* of their laws, which thenceforth were more powerful than any one man. Indeed, the insolence of the last king made this liberty even sweeter.

Tarquin's predecessors had all been praiseworthy rulers who expanded the city and added new homes for the population that they themselves had increased. Though Brutus won true glory by expelling Tarquin, he would have done the public a disservice had he seized power from any of Tarquin's predecessors. In that case, liberty would have come too soon. What would have happened if the hordes of shepherds who made up the plebs would have been given liberty along with their sanctuary? Without the fear of a king, they would have fought with the *patres*, tearing the city in two before the bonds of kinship and love of the land had united the plebs and *patres* into one people. The rule of kings moderated this and brought tranquility. It nurtured Rome until it was ready for liberty, which at the beginning of the republic consisted mainly in the limited term of the consuls. For the consuls were as powerful as the kings, they ruled by the same oaths as the kings, and they carried the same insignia as the kings. The only difference was that they were elected for a year alone, and only one of them was allowed to bear the *fasces*, so as not to double the people's terror. Collatinus allowed Brutus to have the

---

[91] The Assembly of the Centuries was the popular assembly of the time. It had been organized by Servius Tullius.

fasces first, and Brutus was careful to guard the liberty that he had fought so hard to win.

Though the people supported the new constitution, Brutus compelled them to swear an oath that no Roman would ever let a king reign, lest they later be enticed by Tarquin's bribery. He refilled the ranks of the depleted senate with Roman knights, calling the old senators *patres* and the new ones *conscripti*; this brought concord to the city, uniting the patricians and the plebs.

Then he turned his attention to religion. To forestall the need for the king in religious matters, he made a 'little king' to perform all the sacred rites that the Roman kings had previously done in person, but placed him under the power of the high priest, lest the name 'king' threaten Roman liberty.

Indeed, at this point the Romans got a little carried away. The citizens quickly grew jealous of Collatinus himself, who had committed no offense beyond bearing the name Tarquin, for the citizens thought the Tarquins had reigned too long. First there had been Priscus, but the Tarquin claim had not been forgotten during the reign of Servius Tullius, and Tarquin the Proud stole the hereditary kingship back by wickedness and force. Now that Tarquin had been overthrown, the *imperium* was in the hands of Collatinus Tarquin. Because the Romans knew that the Tarquins did not know how to live as private citizens, they considered Collatinus' name itself a threat to their liberty.

The murmuring against Collatinus started gradually and then spread throughout the city. Eventually, Brutus had to call the plebs to a meeting. First, he made them recite the oath promising never to allow a king at Rome nor any man who was a threat to its liberty, to do all in their power to prevent it, and to condemn no action that might avert it.

He proclaimed, "For the love of the republic, I cannot remain silent. I cannot believe that having won your liberty from the Tarquins, you Romans not only let the family remain in the city, but give the *imperium* to one of their line. Does this not put our liberty in danger? Only you, Collatinus Tarquin, can free us from this fear. It is true. Let's confess it. You have helped to throw out the kings. Now, banish their name, the name you yourself bear. Renounce your power. On my authority, you will be provided with whatever you need. Go away, my friend. Free your city from this fear, even though it be an empty one. For your fellow citizens are persuaded that the tyranny of the Tarquins will only depart when all the Tarquins are gone."

The stunned Collatinus said nothing at first. Before he could speak, the nobles who were sitting next to him began to repeat Brutus' demands, which at first did not persuade him. Collatinus was only finally convinced by the entreaties of his father-in-law, Lucretius, who was older and of greater dignity.

Lucretius said to him, "Do what they are asking of you. For it is the will of the people of Rome. You might be banished anyways at the end of your term as consul. If that happens, you will not only lose your homeland, you will lose your goods as well."

So Collatinus abdicated and moved to Lavinium. The Assembly of the Centuries replaced him with Publius Valerius, who had helped to overthrow the king. On the advice of the senate, Brutus exiled all the Tarquins.

Everyone knew that war with the Tarquins was coming, though it did not come as fast as the Romans expected, and they did not foresee the treachery that almost cost them their liberty.

A few of the youths that had once surrounded the Tarquin princes still remained in Rome. These young men had grown accustomed to living licentiously, and now that the law had made everyone equal, they complained that the liberty of others meant slavery for them. A king might be swayed, they reasoned, but the law could not. A king might show mercy to his friends, but the law was deaf and inexorable. The law was more useful for the weak than the powerful. A man who broke it could expect no mercy. Given the errors of human judgment, trying to live by innocence alone was a dangerous proposition.

While this disease was eating away at their souls, the king's ambassadors arrived. These ambassadors said nothing publically about the restoration of the monarchy; they only asked for the return of Tarquin's goods. The senate heard them and consulted on the matter for several days, unsure whether to deny the request and give the Tarquins a cause for war or to grant it and give the Tarquins the means to make war. Meanwhile, the ambassadors were making other plans. While they were openly asking for the return of Tarquin's goods, they were secretly conspiring to return him to power, visiting the city's noble youths, giving them letters from Tarquin, and laying out a plan to admit the former king into the city at night.

Tarquin's ambassadors first approached the Aquilii and Vitellii brothers, the latter of whose sister was married to Brutus and had two adolescent children by him: Titus and Tiberius. Along with a number of other noble youths, these two boys were brought into the conspiracy, under the influence of their uncles.

Meanwhile, the senate had decided to return Tarquin's goods to him, so the ambassadors remained in the city to secure transport, all the while plotting their conspiracy. At last, they convinced the conspirators in Rome to give letters of good faith to Tarquin in order to convince him that their promises were not empty. These letters were a manifest crime, and it was these letters that gave the game away.

On the day before they were to leave, the ambassadors dined with the conspirators at the Vitellii house, and after having dismissed those who were not in on the conspiracy, they laid their final plans. One of the servants in the household was already suspicious but had been waiting to reveal his suspicions until he could prove them. Hearing that the letters had been signed, he immediately took the information to the consuls, who quietly marched to the house, seized the letters, and arrested the traitors. They were in a quandary about what to do with the king's ambassadors. It seemed as if they should be treated as enemies, yet the Romans decided to honor their diplomatic immunity.

The senate angrily decided to reverse its decision, and it distributed the king's goods to the plebs, with the hope that having taken them, the plebs would forever lose any hope of reconciling with him...

Having disposed of Tarquin's goods, they condemned the traitors and carried out their sentences. This was most remarkable because the duties of the consulship forced a father to carry out capital punishment on his own sons. Thus, it was Brutus' fortune to preside over a spectacle that no father should even have to watch. Many of the city's foremost youths stood bound to the stake, but they may as well have been common criminals, for everyone's eyes were on the consul's children. The Romans were not so much distressed by the penalty as by the crime. How could these boys betray their newly-liberated country, their father the liberator, and the consulship that was held by their own family? How could they hand over *patres*, plebs, and all things sacred to an arrogant, exiled, and hostile king?

The consuls sent the lictors to execute the punishment and then sat down in their seats. The boys were stripped nude, beaten with rods, and then decapitated with an axe. Brutus' face betrayed his anguish, but his soul was intent on seeing the punishment carried out.

Cincinnatus

We pick up with Livy's history in 458 BC, fifty-one years after the establishment of the Roman Republic. As the story of Cincinnatus begins, a rival army threatens Rome with destruction.

A great force of Aequians marched nearly to the walls of the city and despoiled the fields. This greatly disturbed the people, and terror overtook the city. Then, the plebs seized their arms, and two large armies were levied...one of which was led by the consul Nautius. Pitching his camp at Eretrum, he led several small expeditions and night raids in which he laid such waste to the enemy's fields that Rome's lands seemed untouched by comparison.

The other army was led by the consul Minucius, who did not have as much luck and did not wage the war with as much vigor. He pitched his camp near the enemy, but feared to leave it, even before any misfortune had befallen him. When the Aequians sensed this fear, they grew bolder. One night, they surrounded the Roman camp and put it under siege, but not before five Roman knights managed to escape and bring the news to Rome, which received it with shock and dismay, almost as if the city itself was besieged. Nautius was summoned home, but he did not seem to be the man to save the city, so the people elected Lucius Quintus Cincinnatus as dictator.[92]

You who care only for riches and think that great honor and virtue must be accompanied with great wealth should listen to this story, for Rome's last hope was a poor farmer who had a mere three acres of land. When the senate's messengers came to him at his farm across the Tiber, he was hard at work, either plowing his fields or digging a ditch.

"*Salve,*" he greeted them, "What service might I be to the republic?"

"Put your toga on," they replied, "and come to the senate. You have been named dictator. Hopefully, this will turn out well for both you and the republic."

Cincinnatus ordered his wife to fetch his toga quickly, and he cleaned his sweaty and grimy face. When he was dressed, the messengers explained the dire situation, congratulated him on being named dictator, and summoned him to the city. He was supplied with a vessel at the public expense, and when he entered Rome, he was greeted by his three sons, some neighbors and friends, and most of the senators. Surrounded by this crowd, the lictors led him to his house. There was also an immense crowd of plebs, who were not happy about the dictator, for they thought that the power granted to Cincinnatus was excessive, and they were afraid of what he might do with it.

Nothing was done that night except keeping watch.

---

[92] In Ancient Rome, the dictatorship was an office that gave the holder absolute power. It was only supposed to be used during emergencies and only supposed to be held for a limited time.

Shortly before dawn the next day, Cincinnatus appointed Lucius Tarquitius as Master of the Horse. Tarquitius was a patrician, but had served as a foot soldier on account of his poverty. Nevertheless, he was considered the best Roman soldier. Cincinnatus entered the forum, proclaimed a cessation of public business, ordered the taverns closed, and forbid the conducting of any private business. He ordered all men of military age to arm themselves, procure five days rations, find twelve large stakes and then come to the Campus Martius before sundown.[93] The older men were to cook food for their younger comrades. Everyone ran here and there, carrying out the dictator's edict.

Cincinnatus drew up his ranks so as to be able to both march and fight if need be, personally leading the legions while Tarquitius led the cavalry. Cincinnatus urged both ranks to move quickly, so that the army might reach the enemy by nightfall.

"The consul and Roman army have been besieged for three days," he warned the soldiers, "and we do not know what another day might bring, for great affairs often hinge on good timing."

The soldiers thus urged each other on. "Hurry, standard bearer," they called.

"Follow, soldiers," he replied.

They reached the enemy in the middle of the night. Then the dictator rode round the enemy camp to see its shape and size as well as he could in the dark. He ordered that the baggage be thrown into one pile and the infantry ready their arms and stakes. The Romans surrounded the enemy camp, then the dictator ordered everyone to make a big war cry, dig a ditch in front of themselves, and fix their stakes. This war cry could be heard in both the enemy camp, where it created great fear, and Minucius' camp, where it created great joy. Seeing that help had come, the besieged Romans ventured out beyond their stations. Minucius thought the battle had already begun, so he ordered his men to take up their arms and follow him.

---

[93] The Campus Martius was the field on the far side of the Tiber on which the Romans performed their military exercises.

Thus, a clamor arose from Minucius' army, and the dictator realized that the fight was on. The Aequians turned to fight Minucius' army in order to prevent them from breaking out; this gave Cincinnatus a free hand, and by dawn, he had the enemy completely surrounded. The Aequians could barely hold up against one army by this point, much less two. At this moment, Cincinnatus attacked and started a second front. Pressed hard on both their interior and exterior, the Aequians asked for terms from the consul, begging to be allowed to retreat. Minucius told them to ask Cincinnatus.

The angry Cincinnatus wanted to shame them, so he ordered their commander and all the other leading men to be led to him in chains and the town of Corbio to be emptied. He did not make the Aequians pay with their blood, but to show that they had been conquered, he made them retreat under a giant yoke constructed out of spears.

The Aequians had left without their baggage, and the Romans found a rich booty in their camp. Cincinnatus gave all the booty to his own soldiers, scolding the consul and his army with these words, "You will get none of this booty, soldiers. You will not make prey of an enemy whose prey you nearly were. And you, Lucius Minucius, until you start acting like a consul, you will command these legions as a staff officer." Minucius gave up his consulship, though Cincinnatus ordered him to remain with the army.

At that time, the Romans were more obedient to authority than they are today, and they valued what Cincinnatus had done for them more than they detested the shame he had imposed on them. Thus, they decreed that the dictator should receive a one-pound crown of gold, and they saluted him as their patron when he left camp. At Rome, Cincinnatus led his ranks in a triumph, with the enemy leaders and standards in front of the chariots and the booty-laden army behind. People laid out suppers for the soldiers, and the suppers were followed by triumphal songs and solemn games. By universal consent, the city gave freedom to Lucius Maximilius Tusculano. The dictator would have immediately laid down his power if it were not for the need to try Marcus Volscius. Fear of the dictator prevented the tribunes from impeding this trial, and Volscius was condemned and sent into exile in Lanuvium. Cincinnatus had been granted dictatorial powers for sixth months, but after sixteen days, he gave up his powers and [returned to his farm].

The Book of Exodus

The accounts of Exodus are impossible to date. Indeed, scholars are divided on the question of whether the Hebrews were ever in Egypt at all. Those scholars who do accept the historicity of the account tend to date Joseph's journey to Egypt sometime between 1750-1500 B.C., but this is impossible to know with any precision. Such a time frame could, however, make Joseph's rise to prominence coincide with the invasion of the Hyksos, a nomadic Semitic people related to the Hebrews who ruled over Egypt beginning in 1630. The subsequent enslavement of the Hebrews might then coincide with the end of Hyksos power in Egypt in 1523 B.C. This would place the Exodus from Egypt sometime between 1500 and 1200 B.C. All of this, however, is simply guesswork.

For centuries, scholars assumed that the book of Exodus, along with the other first five books of the bible, were written by Moses himself. Upon examination of the style of the books, modern scholars have tended to argue that these works were composed by multiple authors over several centuries, many of them probably working from oral traditions.[94]

---

[94] Scripture texts in this work are taken from the *New American Bible, revised edition* © 2010, 1991, 1986, 1970 Confraternity of Christian Doctrine, Washington, D.C. and are used by permission of the copyright owner. All Rights Reserved. No part of the New American Bible may be reproduced in any form without permission in writing from the copyright owner.

Chapter One

¹These are the names of the sons of Israel who, accompanied by their households, entered into Egypt with Jacob: ² Reuben, Simeon, Levi and Judah; ³Issachar, Zebulun and Benjamin; ⁴Dan and Naphtali; Gad and Asher. ⁵The total number of Jacob's direct descendants was seventy. Joseph was already in Egypt.

⁶Now Joseph and all his brothers and that whole generation died. ⁷But the Israelites were fruitful and prolific. They multiplied and became so very numerous that the land was filled with them.

⁸Then a new king, who knew nothing of Joseph, rose to power in Egypt. ⁹He said to his people, "See! The Israelite people have multiplied and become more numerous than we are! ¹⁰Come, let us deal shrewdly with them to stop their increase; otherwise, in time of war they too may join our enemies to fight against us, and so leave the land."

¹¹Accordingly, they set supervisors over the Israelites to oppress them with forced labor. Thus they had to build for Pharaoh the garrison cities of Pithom and Raamses. ¹²Yet the more they were oppressed, the more they multiplied and spread, so that the Egyptians began to loathe the Israelites. ¹³So the Egyptians reduced the Israelites to cruel slavery, ¹⁴making life bitter for them with hard labor, at mortar and brick and all kinds of field work—cruelly oppressed in all their labor.

¹⁵The king of Egypt told the Hebrew midwives, one of whom was called Shiphrah and the other Puah, ¹⁶"When you act as midwives for the Hebrew women, look on the birthstool: if it is a boy, kill him; but if it is a girl, she may live." ¹⁷The midwives, however, feared God; they did not do as the king of Egypt had ordered them, but let the boys live. ¹⁸So the king of Egypt summoned the midwives and asked them, "Why have you done this, allowing the boys to live?" ¹⁹The midwives answered Pharaoh, "The Hebrew women are not like the Egyptian women. They are robust and give birth before the midwife arrives." ²⁰Therefore God dealt well with the midwives; and the people multiplied and grew very numerous. ²¹And because the midwives feared God, God built up families for them. ²²Pharaoh then

commanded all his people, "Throw into the Nile every boy that is born, but you may let all the girls live."

Chapter Two

[1]Now a man of the house of Levi married a Levite woman, [2]and the woman conceived and bore a son. Seeing what a fine child he was, she hid him for three months. [3]But when she could no longer hide him, she took a papyrus basket, daubed it with bitumen and pitch, and putting the child in it, placed it among the reeds on the bank of the Nile. [4]His sister stationed herself at a distance to find out what would happen to him.

[5]Then Pharaoh's daughter came down to bathe at the Nile, while her attendants walked along the bank of the Nile. Noticing the basket among the reeds, she sent her handmaid to fetch it. [6]On opening it, she looked, and there was a baby boy crying! She was moved with pity for him and said, "It is one of the Hebrews' children." [7]Then his sister asked Pharaoh's daughter, "Shall I go and summon a Hebrew woman to nurse the child for you?" [8]Pharaoh's daughter answered her, "Go." So the young woman went and called the child's own mother. [9]Pharaoh's daughter said to her, "Take this child and nurse him for me, and I will pay your wages." So the woman took the child and nursed him. [10]When the child grew, she brought him to Pharaoh's daughter, and he became her son. She named him Moses; for she said, "I drew him out of the water."

[11]On one occasion, after Moses had grown up, when he had gone out to his kinsmen and witnessed their forced labor, he saw an Egyptian striking a Hebrew, one of his own kinsmen. [12]Looking about and seeing no one, he struck down the Egyptian and hid him in the sand. [13]The next day he went out again, and now two Hebrews were fighting! So he asked the culprit, "Why are you striking your companion?" [14]But he replied, "Who has appointed you ruler and judge over us? Are you thinking of killing me as you killed the Egyptian?" Then Moses became afraid and thought, "The affair must certainly be known." [15]When Pharaoh heard of the affair, he sought

to kill Moses. But Moses fled from Pharaoh and went to the land of Midian. There he sat down by a well.

¹⁶Now the priest of Midian had seven daughters, and they came to draw water and fill the troughs to water their father's flock. ¹⁷But shepherds came and drove them away. So Moses rose up in their defense and watered their flock. ¹⁸When they returned to their father Reuel, he said to them, "How is it you have returned so soon today?" ¹⁹They answered, "An Egyptian delivered us from the shepherds. He even drew water for us and watered the flock!" ²⁰"Where is he?" he asked his daughters. "Why did you leave the man there? Invite him to have something to eat." ²¹Moses agreed to stay with him, and the man gave Moses his daughter Zipporah in marriage. ²²She conceived and bore a son, whom he named Gershom; for he said, "I am a stranger residing in a foreign land."

²³A long time passed, during which the king of Egypt died. The Israelites groaned under their bondage and cried out, and from their bondage their cry for help went up to God. ²⁴God heard their moaning and God was mindful of his covenant with Abraham, Isaac and Jacob. ²⁵God saw the Israelites, and God knew….

Chapter Three

¹ Meanwhile Moses was tending the flock of his father-in-law Jethro, the priest of Midian. Leading the flock beyond the wilderness, he came to the mountain of God, Horeb. ²There the angel of the LORD appeared to him as fire flaming out of a bush. When he looked, although the bush was on fire, it was not being consumed. ³So Moses decided, "I must turn aside to look at this remarkable sight. Why does the bush not burn up?" ⁴When the LORD saw that he had turned aside to look, God called out to him from the bush: Moses! Moses! He answered, "Here I am." ⁵God said: Do not come near! Remove your sandals from your feet, for the place where you stand is holy ground. ⁶I am the God of your father, he continued, the God of Abraham, the God of Isaac, and the God of Jacob. Moses hid his face, for he was afraid to look at God.

⁷But the LORD said: I have witnessed the affliction of my people in Egypt and have heard their cry against their taskmasters, so I know well what they are suffering. ⁸Therefore I have come down to rescue them from the power of the Egyptians and lead them up from that land into a good and spacious land, a land flowing with milk and honey, the country of the Canaanites, the Hittites, the Amorites, the Perizzites, the Girgashites, the Hivites and the Jebusites. ⁹Now indeed the outcry of the Israelites has reached me, and I have seen how the Egyptians are oppressing them. ¹⁰Now, go! I am sending you to Pharaoh to bring my people, the Israelites, out of Egypt.

¹¹But Moses said to God, "Who am I that I should go to Pharaoh and bring the Israelites out of Egypt?" ¹²God answered: I will be with you; and this will be your sign that I have sent you. When you have brought the people out of Egypt, you will serve God at this mountain. ¹³"But," said Moses to God, "if I go to the Israelites and say to them, 'The God of your ancestors has sent me to you,' and they ask me, 'What is his name?' what do I tell them?" ¹⁴God replied to Moses: I am who I am. Then he added: This is what you will tell the Israelites: I AM has sent me to you.

¹⁵God spoke further to Moses: This is what you will say to the Israelites: The LORD, the God of your ancestors, the God of Abraham, the God of Isaac, and the God of Jacob, has sent me to you. This is my name forever; this is my title for all generations.

¹⁶Go and gather the elders of the Israelites, and tell them, The LORD, the God of your ancestors, the God of Abraham, Isaac, and Jacob, has appeared to me and said: I have observed you and what is being done to you in Egypt; ¹⁷so I have decided to lead you up out of your affliction in Egypt into the land of the Canaanites, the Hittites, the Amorites, the Perizzites, the Girgashites, the Hivites and the Jebusites, a land flowing with milk and honey. ¹⁸They will listen to you. Then you and the elders of Israel will go to the king of Egypt and say to him: The LORD, the God of the Hebrews, has come to meet us. So now, let us go a three days' journey in the wilderness to offer sacrifice to the LORD, our God. ¹⁹Yet I know that the king of Egypt will not allow you to go unless his hand is forced. ²⁰So I will

stretch out my hand and strike Egypt with all the wondrous deeds I will do in its midst. After that he will let you go. ²¹ I will even make the Egyptians so well-disposed toward this people that, when you go, you will not go empty-handed. ²²Every woman will ask her neighbor and the resident alien in her house for silver and gold articles and for clothing, and you will put them on your sons and daughters. So you will plunder the Egyptians.

Chapter Four

¹"But," objected Moses, "suppose they do not believe me or listen to me? For they may say, 'The LORD did not appear to you.'" ²The LORD said to him: What is in your hand? "A staff," he answered. ³God said: Throw it on the ground. So he threw it on the ground and it became a snake, and Moses backed away from it. ⁴Then the LORD said to Moses: Now stretch out your hand and take hold of its tail. So he stretched out his hand and took hold of it, and it became a staff in his hand. ⁵That is so they will believe that the LORD, the God of their ancestors, the God of Abraham, the God of Isaac, and the God of Jacob, did appear to you.

⁶Again the LORD said to him: Put your hand into the fold of your garment. So he put his hand into the fold of his garment, and when he drew it out, there was his hand covered with scales, like snowflakes. ⁷Then God said: Put your hand back into the fold of your garment. So he put his hand back into the fold of his garment, and when he drew it out, there it was again like his own flesh. ⁸If they do not believe you or pay attention to the message of the first sign, they should believe the message of the second sign. ⁹And if they do not believe even these two signs and do not listen to you, take some water from the Nile and pour it on the dry land. The water you take from the Nile will become blood on the dry land.

¹⁰Moses, however, said to the LORD, "If you please, my Lord, I have never been eloquent, neither in the past nor now that you have spoken to your servant; but I am slow of speech and tongue." ¹¹The LORD said to him: Who gives one person speech? Who makes

another mute or deaf, seeing or blind? Is it not I, the LORD? ¹²Now go, I will assist you in speaking and teach you what you are to say. ¹³But he said, "If you please, my Lord, send someone else!" ¹⁴Then the LORD became angry with Moses and said: I know there is your brother, Aaron the Levite, who is a good speaker; even now he is on his way to meet you. When he sees you, he will truly be glad. ¹⁵You will speak to him and put the words in his mouth. I will assist both you and him in speaking and teach you both what you are to do. ¹⁶He will speak to the people for you: he will be your spokesman, and you will be as God to him. ¹⁷Take this staff in your hand; with it you are to perform the signs.

¹⁸After this Moses returned to Jethro his father-in-law and said to him, "Let me return to my kindred in Egypt, to see whether they are still living." Jethro replied to Moses, "Go in peace." ¹⁹Then the LORD said to Moses in Midian: Return to Egypt, for all those who sought your life are dead. ²⁰So Moses took his wife and his sons, mounted them on the donkey, and started back to the land of Egypt. Moses took the staff of God with him. ²¹The LORD said to Moses: On your return to Egypt, see that you perform before Pharaoh all the wonders I have put in your power. But I will harden his heart and he will not let the people go. ²² So you will say to Pharaoh, Thus says the LORD: Israel is my son, my firstborn. ²³I said to you: Let my son go, that he may serve me. Since you refused to let him go, I will kill your son, your firstborn.

²⁴On the journey, at a place where they spent the night, the LORD came upon Moses and sought to put him to death. ²⁵ But Zipporah took a piece of flint and cut off her son's foreskin and, touching his feet, she said, "Surely you are a spouse of blood to me." ²⁶So God let Moses alone. At that time she said, "A spouse of blood," in regard to the circumcision.

²⁷The LORD said to Aaron: Go into the wilderness to meet Moses. So he went; when meeting him at the mountain of God, he kissed him. ²⁸Moses told Aaron everything the LORD had sent him to say, and all the signs he had commanded him to do. ²⁹Then Moses and Aaron went and gathered all the elders of the Israelites. ³⁰Aaron told

them everything the LORD had said to Moses, and he performed the signs before the people. ³¹The people believed, and when they heard that the LORD had observed the Israelites and had seen their affliction, they knelt and bowed down.

In chapters 5-11, God sends several plagues upon the Egyptians, but each time pharoah's heart is hardened and he refuses to let the Israelites go. We pick back up with the story in chapter twelve with the final plague: the death of the firstborn.

Chapter Twelve

¹The LORD said to Moses and Aaron in the land of Egypt: ² This month will stand at the head of your calendar; you will reckon it the first month of the year. ³Tell the whole community of Israel: On the tenth of this month every family must procure for itself a lamb, one apiece for each household. ⁴If a household is too small for a lamb, it along with its nearest neighbor will procure one, and apportion the lamb's cost in proportion to the number of persons, according to what each household consumes. ⁵Your lamb must be a year-old male and without blemish. You may take it from either the sheep or the goats. ⁶You will keep it until the fourteenth day of this month, and then, with the whole community of Israel assembled, it will be slaughtered during the evening twilight. ⁷They will take some of its blood and apply it to the two doorposts and the lintel of the houses in which they eat it. ⁸They will consume its meat that same night, eating it roasted with unleavened bread and bitter herbs. ⁹Do not eat any of it raw or even boiled in water, but roasted, with its head and shanks and inner organs. ¹⁰You must not keep any of it beyond the morning; whatever is left over in the morning must be burned up.

¹¹This is how you are to eat it: with your loins girt, sandals on your feet and your staff in hand, you will eat it in a hurry. It is the LORD's Passover. ¹²For on this same night I will go through Egypt, striking down every firstborn in the land, human being and beast

alike, and executing judgment on all the gods of Egypt—I, the LORD! ¹³But for you the blood will mark the houses where you are. Seeing the blood, I will pass over you; thereby, when I strike the land of Egypt, no destructive blow will come upon you.

¹⁴This day will be a day of remembrance for you, which your future generations will celebrate with pilgrimage to the LORD; you will celebrate it as a statute forever. ¹⁵For seven days you must eat unleavened bread. From the very first day you will have your houses clear of all leaven. For whoever eats leavened bread from the first day to the seventh will be cut off from Israel. ¹⁶On the first day you will hold a sacred assembly, and likewise on the seventh. On these days no sort of work shall be done, except to prepare the food that everyone needs. ¹⁷Keep, then, the custom of the unleavened bread, since it was on this very day that I brought your armies out of the land of Egypt. You must observe this day throughout your generations as a statute forever. ¹⁸From the evening of the fourteenth day of the first month until the evening of the twenty-first day of this month you will eat unleavened bread. ¹⁹For seven days no leaven may be found in your houses; for anyone, a resident alien or a native, who eats leavened food will be cut off from the community of Israel. ²⁰You shall eat nothing leavened; wherever you dwell you may eat only unleavened bread.

²¹Moses summoned all the elders of Israel and said to them, "Go and procure lambs for your families, and slaughter the Passover victims. ²² Then take a bunch of hyssop, and dipping it in the blood that is in the basin, apply some of this blood to the lintel and the two doorposts. And none of you shall go outdoors until morning. ²³For when the LORD goes by to strike down the Egyptians, seeing the blood on the lintel and the two doorposts, the LORD will pass over that door and not let the destroyer come into your houses to strike you down.

²⁴"You will keep this practice forever as a statute for yourselves and your descendants. ²⁵Thus, when you have entered the land which the LORD will give you as he promised, you must observe this rite. ²⁶ When your children ask you, 'What does this rite of yours

mean?' ²⁷you will reply, 'It is the Passover sacrifice for the LORD, who passed over the houses of the Israelites in Egypt; when he struck down the Egyptians, he delivered our houses.'"

Then the people knelt and bowed down, ²⁸and the Israelites went and did exactly as the LORD had commanded Moses and Aaron.

²⁹And so at midnight the LORD struck down every firstborn in the land of Egypt, from the firstborn of Pharaoh sitting on his throne to the firstborn of the prisoner in the dungeon, as well as all the firstborn of the animals. ³⁰Pharaoh arose in the night, he and all his servants and all the Egyptians; and there was loud wailing throughout Egypt, for there was not a house without its dead.

³¹During the night Pharaoh summoned Moses and Aaron and said, "Leave my people at once, you and the Israelites! Go and serve the LORD as you said. ³²Take your flocks, too, and your herds, as you said, and go; and bless me, too!"

³³The Egyptians, in a hurry to send them away from the land, urged the people on, for they said, "All of us will die!" ³⁴The people, therefore, took their dough before it was leavened, in their kneading bowls wrapped in their cloaks on their shoulders. ³⁵ And the Israelites did as Moses had commanded: they asked the Egyptians for articles of silver and gold and for clothing. ³⁶Indeed the LORD had made the Egyptians so well-disposed toward the people that they let them have whatever they asked for. And so they despoiled the Egyptians.

³⁷The Israelites set out from Rameses for Succoth, about six hundred thousand men on foot, not counting the children. ³⁸A crowd of mixed ancestry also went up with them, with livestock in great abundance, both flocks and herds. ³⁹The dough they had brought out of Egypt they baked into unleavened loaves. It was not leavened, because they had been driven out of Egypt and could not wait. They did not even prepare food for the journey.

⁴⁰The time the Israelites had stayed in Egypt was four hundred and thirty years. ⁴¹At the end of four hundred and thirty years, on this very date, all the armies of the LORD left the land of Egypt. ⁴²This was a night of vigil for the LORD, when he brought them out of the

land of Egypt; so on this night all Israelites must keep a vigil for the LORD throughout their generations.

⁴³The LORD said to Moses and Aaron: This is the Passover statute. No foreigner may eat of it. ⁴⁴However, every slave bought for money you will circumcise; then he may eat of it. ⁴⁵But no tenant or hired worker may eat of it. ⁴⁶It must be eaten in one house; you may not take any of its meat outside the house. You shall not break any of its bones. ⁴⁷The whole community of Israel must celebrate this feast. ⁴⁸If any alien residing among you would celebrate the Passover for the LORD, all his males must be circumcised, and then he may join in its celebration just like the natives. But no one who is uncircumcised may eat of it. ⁴⁹There will be one law for the native and for the alien residing among you.

⁵⁰All the Israelites did exactly as the LORD had commanded Moses and Aaron. ⁵¹On that same day the LORD brought the Israelites out of the land of Egypt company by company.

Chapter Thirteen

¹The LORD spoke to Moses and said: ²Consecrate to me every firstborn; whatever opens the womb among the Israelites, whether of human being or beast, belongs to me.

³ Moses said to the people, "Remember this day on which you came out of Egypt, out of a house of slavery. For it was with a strong hand that the LORD brought you out from there. Nothing made with leaven may be eaten. ⁴This day on which you are going out is in the month of Abib. ⁵Therefore, when the LORD, your God, has brought you into the land of the Canaanites, the Hittites, the Amorites, the Perrizites, the Girgashites, the Hivites, and the Jebusites, which he swore to your ancestors to give you, a land flowing with milk and honey, you will perform the following service in this month. ⁶For seven days you will eat unleavened bread, and the seventh day will also be a festival to the LORD. ⁷Unleavened bread may be eaten during the seven days, but nothing leavened and no leaven may be found in your possession in all your territory. ⁸And on that day you

will explain to your son, 'This is because of what the LORD did for me when I came out of Egypt.' ⁹It will be like a sign on your hand and a reminder on your forehead, so that the teaching of the LORD will be on your lips: with a strong hand the LORD brought you out of Egypt. ¹⁰You will keep this statute at its appointed time from year to year.

¹¹"When the LORD, your God, has brought you into the land of the Canaanites, just as he swore to you and your ancestors, and gives it to you, ¹² you will dedicate to the LORD every newborn that opens the womb; and every firstborn male of your animals will belong to the LORD. ¹³Every firstborn of a donkey you will ransom with a sheep. If you do not ransom it, you will break its neck. Every human firstborn of your sons you must ransom. ¹⁴And when your son asks you later on, 'What does this mean?' you will tell him, 'With a strong hand the LORD brought us out of Egypt, out of a house of slavery. ¹⁵When Pharaoh stubbornly refused to let us go, the LORD killed every firstborn in the land of Egypt, the firstborn of human being and beast alike. That is why I sacrifice to the LORD every male that opens the womb, and why I ransom every firstborn of my sons.' ¹⁶It will be like a sign on your hand and a band on your forehead that with a strong hand the LORD brought us out of Egypt."

¹⁷Now, when Pharaoh let the people go, God did not lead them by way of the Philistines' land, though this was the nearest; for God said: If the people see that they have to fight, they might change their minds and return to Egypt. ¹⁸Instead, God rerouted them toward the Red Sea by way of the wilderness road, and the Israelites went up out of the land of Egypt arrayed for battle. ¹⁹Moses also took Joseph's bones with him, for Joseph had made the Israelites take a solemn oath, saying, "God will surely take care of you, and you must bring my bones up with you from here."

²⁰Setting out from Succoth, they camped at Etham near the edge of the wilderness.

²¹The LORD preceded them, in the daytime by means of a column of cloud to show them the way, and at night by means of a column of fire to give them light. Thus they could travel both day and night.

²²Neither the column of cloud by day nor the column of fire by night ever left its place in front of the people.

Chapter Fourteen

¹Then the LORD spoke to Moses: ²Speak to the Israelites: Let them turn about and camp before Pi-hahiroth, between Migdol and the sea. Camp in front of Baal-zephon, just opposite, by the sea. ³Pharaoh will then say, "The Israelites are wandering about aimlessly in the land. The wilderness has closed in on them." ⁴I will so harden Pharaoh's heart that he will pursue them. Thus I will receive glory through Pharaoh and all his army, and the Egyptians will know that I am the LORD.

This the Israelites did. ⁵ When it was reported to the king of Egypt that the people had fled, Pharaoh and his servants had a change of heart about the people. "What in the world have we done!" they said. "We have released Israel from our service!" ⁶So Pharaoh harnessed his chariots and took his army with him. ⁷He took six hundred select chariots and all the chariots of Egypt, with officers on all of them. ⁸The LORD hardened the heart of Pharaoh, king of Egypt, so that he pursued the Israelites while they were going out in triumph. ⁹The Egyptians pursued them—all Pharaoh's horses, his chariots, his horsemen, and his army—and caught up with them as they lay encamped by the sea, at Pi-hahiroth, in front of Baal-zephon.

¹⁰Now Pharaoh was near when the Israelites looked up and saw that the Egyptians had set out after them. Greatly frightened, the Israelites cried out to the LORD. ¹¹To Moses they said, "Were there no burial places in Egypt that you brought us to die in the wilderness? What have you done to us, bringing us out of Egypt? ¹²Did we not tell you this in Egypt, when we said, 'Leave us alone that we may serve the Egyptians'? Far better for us to serve the Egyptians than to die in the wilderness." ¹³But Moses answered the people, "Do not fear! Stand your ground and see the victory the LORD will win for you today. For these Egyptians whom you see

today you will never see again. ¹⁴The LORD will fight for you; you have only to keep still."

¹⁵Then the LORD said to Moses: Why are you crying out to me? Tell the Israelites to set out. ¹⁶And you, lift up your staff and stretch out your hand over the sea, and split it in two, that the Israelites may pass through the sea on dry land. ¹⁷But I will harden the hearts of the Egyptians so that they will go in after them, and I will receive glory through Pharaoh and all his army, his chariots and his horsemen. ¹⁸The Egyptians will know that I am the LORD, when I receive glory through Pharaoh, his chariots, and his horsemen.

¹⁹The angel of God, who had been leading Israel's army, now moved and went around behind them. And the column of cloud, moving from in front of them, took up its place behind them, ²⁰so that it came between the Egyptian army and that of Israel. And when it became dark, the cloud illumined the night; and so the rival camps did not come any closer together all night long. ²¹ Then Moses stretched out his hand over the sea; and the LORD drove back the sea with a strong east wind all night long and turned the sea into dry ground. The waters were split, ²²so that the Israelites entered into the midst of the sea on dry land, with the water as a wall to their right and to their left.

²³The Egyptians followed in pursuit after them—all Pharaoh's horses and chariots and horsemen—into the midst of the sea. ²⁴But during the watch just before dawn, the LORD looked down from a column of fiery cloud upon the Egyptian army and threw it into a panic; ²⁵and he so clogged their chariot wheels that they could drive only with difficulty. With that the Egyptians said, "Let us flee from Israel, because the LORD is fighting for them against Egypt."

²⁶Then the LORD spoke to Moses: Stretch out your hand over the sea, that the water may flow back upon the Egyptians, upon their chariots and their horsemen. ²⁷So Moses stretched out his hand over the sea, and at daybreak the sea returned to its normal flow. The Egyptians were fleeing head on toward it when the LORD cast the Egyptians into the midst of the sea. ²⁸ As the water flowed back, it covered the chariots and the horsemen. Of all Pharaoh's army which

had followed the Israelites into the sea, not even one escaped. ²⁹But the Israelites had walked on dry land through the midst of the sea, with the water as a wall to their right and to their left. ³⁰Thus the LORD saved Israel on that day from the power of Egypt. When Israel saw the Egyptians lying dead on the seashore ³¹and saw the great power that the LORD had shown against Egypt, the people feared the LORD. They believed in the LORD and in Moses his servant.

Chapter Fifteen

¹Then Moses and the Israelites sang this song to the LORD:

I will sing to the LORD, for he is gloriously triumphant;
horse and chariot he has cast into the sea.
²My strength and my refuge is the LORD,
and he has become my savior.
This is my God, I praise him;
the God of my father, I extol him.
³The LORD is a warrior,
LORD is his name!
⁴Pharaoh's chariots and army he hurled into the sea;
the elite of his officers were drowned in the Red Sea.
⁵The flood waters covered them,
they sank into the depths like a stone.
⁶Your right hand, O LORD, magnificent in power,
your right hand, O LORD, shattered the enemy.
⁷In your great majesty you overthrew your adversaries;
you loosed your wrath to consume them like stubble.
⁸At the blast of your nostrils the waters piled up,
the flowing waters stood like a mound,
the flood waters foamed in the midst of the sea.
⁹The enemy boasted, "I will pursue and overtake them;
I will divide the spoils and have my fill of them;
I will draw my sword; my hand will despoil them!"
¹⁰When you blew with your breath, the sea covered them;

like lead they sank in the mighty waters.
[11]Who is like you among the gods, O LORD?
Who is like you, magnificent among the holy ones?
Awe-inspiring in deeds of renown, worker of wonders,
  [12]when you stretched out your right hand, the earth swallowed
  them!
[13]In your love you led the people you redeemed;
in your strength you guided them to your holy dwelling.
[14]The peoples heard and quaked;
anguish gripped the dwellers in Philistia.
[15]Then were the chieftains of Edom dismayed,
the nobles of Moab seized by trembling;
All the inhabitants of Canaan melted away;
[16] terror and dread fell upon them.
By the might of your arm they became silent like stone,
while your people, LORD, passed over,
while the people whom you created passed over.
[17]You brought them in, you planted them
on the mountain that is your own —
The place you made the base of your throne, LORD,
the sanctuary, LORD, your hands established.
[18]May the LORD reign forever and ever!

[19]When Pharaoh's horses and chariots and horsemen entered the sea, the LORD made the waters of the sea flow back upon them, though the Israelites walked on dry land through the midst of the sea.

[20]Then the prophet Miriam, Aaron's sister, took a tambourine in her hand, while all the women went out after her with tambourines, dancing; [21]and she responded to them:

Sing to the LORD, for he is gloriously triumphant;
horse and chariot he has cast into the sea.

²² Then Moses led Israel forward from the Red Sea, and they marched out to the wilderness of Shur. After traveling for three days through the wilderness without finding water, ²³they arrived at Marah, where they could not drink its water, because it was too bitter. Hence this place was called Marah. ²⁴As the people grumbled against Moses, saying, "What are we to drink?" ²⁵he cried out to the LORD, who pointed out to him a piece of wood. When he threw it into the water, the water became fresh.

It was here that God, in making statutes and ordinances for them, put them to the test. ²⁶He said: If you listen closely to the voice of the LORD, your God, and do what is right in his eyes: if you heed his commandments and keep all his statutes, I will not afflict you with any of the diseases with which I afflicted the Egyptians; for I, the LORD, am your healer.

²⁷Then they came to Elim, where there were twelve springs of water and seventy palm trees, and they camped there near the water.

Chapter Sixteen

¹Having set out from Elim, the whole Israelite community came into the wilderness of Sin, which is between Elim and Sinai, on the fifteenth day of the second month after their departure from the land of Egypt. ²Here in the wilderness the whole Israelite community grumbled against Moses and Aaron. ³The Israelites said to them, "If only we had died at the LORD's hand in the land of Egypt, as we sat by our kettles of meat and ate our fill of bread! But you have led us into this wilderness to make this whole assembly die of famine!"

⁴Then the LORD said to Moses: I am going to rain down bread from heaven for you. Each day the people are to go out and gather their daily portion; thus will I test them, to see whether they follow my instructions or not. ⁵On the sixth day, however, when they prepare what they bring in, let it be twice as much as they gather on the other days. ⁶So Moses and Aaron told all the Israelites, "At evening you will know that it was the LORD who brought you out of the land of Egypt; ⁷and in the morning you will see the glory of the

LORD, when he hears your grumbling against him. But who are we that you should grumble against us?" [8]And Moses said, "When the LORD gives you meat to eat in the evening and in the morning your fill of bread, and hears the grumbling you utter against him, who then are we? Your grumbling is not against us, but against the LORD."

[9]Then Moses said to Aaron, "Tell the whole Israelite community: Approach the LORD, for he has heard your grumbling." [10]But while Aaron was speaking to the whole Israelite community, they turned in the direction of the wilderness, and there the glory of the LORD appeared in the cloud! [11]The LORD said to Moses: [12]I have heard the grumbling of the Israelites. Tell them: In the evening twilight you will eat meat, and in the morning you will have your fill of bread, and then you will know that I, the LORD, am your God.

[13]In the evening, quail came up and covered the camp. In the morning there was a layer of dew all about the camp, [14]and when the layer of dew evaporated, fine flakes were on the surface of the wilderness, fine flakes like hoarfrost on the ground. [15]On seeing it, the Israelites asked one another, "What is this?" for they did not know what it was. But Moses told them, "It is the bread which the LORD has given you to eat.

[16]"Now, this is what the LORD has commanded. Gather as much of it as each needs to eat, an omer for each person for as many of you as there are, each of you providing for those in your own tent." [17]The Israelites did so. Some gathered a large and some a small amount. [18] But when they measured it out by the omer, the one who had gathered a large amount did not have too much, and the one who had gathered a small amount did not have too little. They gathered as much as each needed to eat. [19]Moses said to them, "Let no one leave any of it over until morning." [20]But they did not listen to Moses, and some kept a part of it over until morning, and it became wormy and stank. Therefore Moses was angry with them.

[21]Morning after morning they gathered it, as much as each needed to eat; but when the sun grew hot, it melted away. [22]On the sixth day they gathered twice as much food, two omers for each

person. When all the leaders of the community came and reported this to Moses, [23]he told them, "That is what the LORD has prescribed. Tomorrow is a day of rest, a holy sabbath of the LORD. Whatever you want to bake, bake; whatever you want to boil, boil; but whatever is left put away and keep until the morning." [24]When they put it away until the morning, as Moses commanded, it did not stink nor were there worms in it. [25]Moses then said, "Eat it today, for today is the sabbath of the LORD. Today you will not find any in the field. [26]Six days you will gather it, but on the seventh day, the sabbath, it will not be there." [27]Still, on the seventh day some of the people went out to gather it, but they did not find any. [28]Then the LORD said to Moses: How long will you refuse to keep my commandments and my instructions? [29]Take note! The LORD has given you the sabbath. That is why on the sixth day he gives you food for two days. Each of you stay where you are and let no one go out on the seventh day. [30]After that the people rested on the seventh day.

[31]The house of Israel named this food manna. It was like coriander seed, white, and it tasted like wafers made with honey.

[32]Moses said, "This is what the LORD has commanded. Keep a full omer of it for your future generations, so that they may see the food I gave you to eat in the wilderness when I brought you out of the land of Egypt." [33]Moses then told Aaron, "Take a jar and put a full omer of manna in it. Then place it before the LORD to keep it for your future generations." [34]As the LORD had commanded Moses, Aaron placed it in front of the covenant to keep it.

[35]The Israelites ate the manna for forty years, until they came to settled land; they ate the manna until they came to the borders of Canaan. [36](An omer is one tenth of an ephah.)

Chapter Seventeen

[1]From the wilderness of Sin the whole Israelite community journeyed by stages, as the LORD directed, and encamped at Rephidim.

But there was no water for the people to drink, ² and so they quarreled with Moses and said, "Give us water to drink." Moses replied to them, "Why do you quarrel with me? Why do you put the LORD to a test?" ³Here, then, in their thirst for water, the people grumbled against Moses, saying, "Why then did you bring us up out of Egypt? To have us die of thirst with our children and our livestock?" ⁴So Moses cried out to the LORD, "What shall I do with this people? A little more and they will stone me!" ⁵The LORD answered Moses: Go on ahead of the people, and take along with you some of the elders of Israel, holding in your hand, as you go, the staff with which you struck the Nile. ⁶I will be standing there in front of you on the rock in Horeb. Strike the rock, and the water will flow from it for the people to drink. Moses did this, in the sight of the elders of Israel. ⁷The place was named Massah and Meribah, because the Israelites quarreled there and tested the LORD, saying, "Is the LORD in our midst or not?"

⁸Then Amalek came and waged war against Israel in Rephidim. ⁹So Moses said to Joshua, "Choose some men for us, and tomorrow go out and engage Amalek in battle. I will be standing on top of the hill with the staff of God in my hand." ¹⁰Joshua did as Moses told him: he engaged Amalek in battle while Moses, Aaron, and Hur climbed to the top of the hill. ¹¹As long as Moses kept his hands raised up, Israel had the better of the fight, but when he let his hands rest, Amalek had the better of the fight. ¹²Moses' hands, however, grew tired; so they took a rock and put it under him and he sat on it. Meanwhile Aaron and Hur supported his hands, one on one side and one on the other, so that his hands remained steady until sunset. ¹³And Joshua defeated Amalek and his people with the sword.

¹⁴Then the LORD said to Moses: Write this down in a book as something to be remembered, and recite it to Joshua: I will completely blot out the memory of Amalek from under the heavens. ¹⁵Moses built an altar there, which he named Yahweh-nissi; ¹⁶for he said, "Take up the banner of the LORD! The LORD has a war against Amalek through the ages."

Chapter Eighteen

¹Now Moses' father-in-law Jethro, the priest of Midian, heard of all that God had done for Moses and for his people Israel: how the LORD had brought Israel out of Egypt. ²So his father-in-law Jethro took along Zipporah, Moses' wife—now this was after Moses had sent her back— ³and her two sons. One of these was named Gershom; for he said, "I am a resident alien in a foreign land." ⁴The other was named Eliezer; for he said, "The God of my father is my help; he has rescued me from Pharaoh's sword." ⁵Together with Moses' wife and sons, then, his father-in-law Jethro came to him in the wilderness where he was encamped at the mountain of God, ⁶and he sent word to Moses, "I, your father-in-law Jethro, am coming to you, along with your wife and her two sons."

⁷Moses went out to meet his father-in-law, bowed down, and then kissed him. Having greeted each other, they went into the tent. ⁸Moses then told his father-in-law of all that the LORD had done to Pharaoh and the Egyptians for the sake of Israel, and of all the hardships that had beset them on their journey, and how the LORD had rescued them. ⁹Jethro rejoiced over all the goodness that the LORD had shown Israel in rescuing them from the power of the Egyptians. ¹⁰"Blessed be the LORD," he said, "who has rescued you from the power of the Egyptians and of Pharaoh. ¹¹Now I know that the LORD is greater than all the gods; for he rescued the people from the power of the Egyptians when they treated them arrogantly." ¹²Then Jethro, the father-in-law of Moses, brought a burnt offering and sacrifices for God, and Aaron came with all the elders of Israel to share with Moses' father-in-law in the meal before God.

¹³The next day Moses sat in judgment for the people, while they stood around him from morning until evening. ¹⁴When Moses' father-in-law saw all that he was doing for the people, he asked, "What is this business that you are conducting for the people? Why do you sit alone while all the people have to stand about you from morning till evening?" ¹⁵Moses answered his father-in-law, "The people come to me to consult God. ¹⁶Whenever they have a

disagreement, they come to me to have me settle the matter between them and make known to them God's statutes and instructions."

¹⁷"What you are doing is not wise," Moses' father-in-law replied. ¹⁸"You will surely wear yourself out, both you and these people with you. The task is too heavy for you; you cannot do it alone. ¹⁹ Now, listen to me, and I will give you some advice, and may God be with you. Act as the people's representative before God, and bring their disputes to God. ²⁰Enlighten them in regard to the statutes and instructions, showing them how they are to conduct themselves and what they are to do. ²¹But you should also look among all the people for able and God-fearing men, trustworthy men who hate dishonest gain, and set them over the people as commanders of thousands, of hundreds, of fifties, and of tens. ²²Let these render decisions for the people in all routine cases. Every important case they should refer to you, but every lesser case they can settle themselves. Lighten your burden by letting them bear it with you! ²³If you do this, and God so commands you, you will be able to stand the strain, and all these people, too, will go home content."

²⁴Moses listened to his father-in-law and did all that he had said. ²⁵He picked out able men from all Israel and put them in charge of the people as commanders of thousands, of hundreds, of fifties, and of tens. ²⁶They rendered decisions for the people in all routine cases. The more difficult cases they referred to Moses, but all the lesser cases they settled themselves. ²⁷Then Moses said farewell to his father-in-law, who went off to his own country.

Chapter Nineteen

¹ In the third month after the Israelites' departure from the land of Egypt, on the first day, they came to the wilderness of Sinai. ²After they made the journey from Rephidim and entered the wilderness of Sinai, they then pitched camp in the wilderness.

While Israel was encamped there in front of the mountain, ³Moses went up to the mountain of God. Then the LORD called to him from the mountain, saying: This is what you will say to the house of Jacob; tell the Israelites: ⁴You have seen how I treated the Egyptians and how I bore you up on eagles' wings and brought you to myself. ⁵Now, if you obey me completely and keep my covenant, you will be my treasured possession among all peoples, though all the earth is mine. ⁶You will be to me a kingdom of priests, a holy nation. That is what you must tell the Israelites. ⁷So Moses went and summoned the elders of the people. When he set before them all that the LORD had ordered him to tell them, ⁸all the people answered together, "Everything the LORD has said, we will do." Then Moses brought back to the LORD the response of the people.

⁹The LORD said to Moses: I am coming to you now in a dense cloud, so that when the people hear me speaking with you, they will also remain faithful to you.

When Moses, then, had reported the response of the people to the LORD, ¹⁰the LORD said to Moses: Go to the people and have them sanctify themselves today and tomorrow. Have them wash their garments ¹¹and be ready for the third day; for on the third day the LORD will come down on Mount Sinai in the sight of all the people. ¹²Set limits for the people all around, saying: Take care not to go up the mountain, or even to touch its edge. All who touch the mountain must be put to death. ¹³No hand shall touch them, but they must be stoned to death or killed with arrows. Whether human being or beast, they must not be allowed to live. Only when the ram's horn sounds may they go up on the mountain. ¹⁴Then Moses came down from the mountain to the people and had them sanctify themselves, and they washed their garments. ¹⁵He said to the people, "Be ready for the third day. Do not approach a woman."

¹⁶ On the morning of the third day there were peals of thunder and lightning, and a heavy cloud over the mountain, and a very loud blast of the shofar, so that all the people in the camp trembled. ¹⁷But Moses led the people out of the camp to meet God, and they stationed themselves at the foot of the mountain. ¹⁸Now Mount Sinai was completely enveloped in smoke, because the LORD had come down upon it in fire. The smoke rose from it as though from a kiln, and the whole mountain trembled violently. ¹⁹The blast of the shofar grew

louder and louder, while Moses was speaking and God was answering him with thunder.

²⁰When the LORD came down upon Mount Sinai, to the top of the mountain, the LORD summoned Moses to the top of the mountain, and Moses went up. ²¹Then the LORD told Moses: Go down and warn the people not to break through to the LORD in order to see him; otherwise many of them will be struck down. ²²For their part, the priests, who approach the LORD must sanctify themselves; else the LORD will break out in anger against them. ²³But Moses said to the LORD, "The people cannot go up to Mount Sinai, for you yourself warned us, saying: Set limits around the mountain to make it sacred." ²⁴So the LORD said to him: Go down and come up along with Aaron. But do not let the priests and the people break through to come up to the LORD; else he will break out against them." ²⁵So Moses went down to the people and spoke to them.

Chapter Twenty

¹Then God spoke all these words:

² I am the LORD your God, who brought you out of the land of Egypt, out of the house of slavery. ³You shall not have other gods beside me. ⁴You shall not make for yourself an idol or a likeness of anything in the heavens above or on the earth below or in the waters beneath the earth; ⁵you shall not bow down before them or serve them. For I, the LORD, your God, am a jealous God, inflicting punishment for their ancestors' wickedness on the children of those who hate me, down to the third and fourth generation; ⁶but showing love down to the thousandth generation of those who love me and keep my commandments.

⁷You shall not invoke the name of the LORD, your God, in vain. For the LORD will not leave unpunished anyone who invokes his name in vain.

⁸Remember the sabbath day—keep it holy. ⁹Six days you may labor and do all your work, ¹⁰but the seventh day is a sabbath of the LORD your God. You shall not do any work, either you, your son or

your daughter, your male or female slave, your work animal, or the resident alien within your gates. ¹¹For in six days the LORD made the heavens and the earth, the sea and all that is in them; but on the seventh day he rested. That is why the LORD has blessed the sabbath day and made it holy.

¹²Honor your father and your mother, that you may have a long life in the land the LORD your God is giving you.

¹³You shall not kill.

¹⁴You shall not commit adultery.

¹⁵You shall not steal.

¹⁶You shall not bear false witness against your neighbor.

¹⁷You shall not covet your neighbor's house. You shall not covet your neighbor's wife, his male or female slave, his ox or donkey, or anything that belongs to your neighbor.

¹⁸Now as all the people witnessed the thunder and lightning, the blast of the shofar and the mountain smoking, they became afraid and trembled. So they took up a position farther away ¹⁹and said to Moses, "You speak to us, and we will listen; but do not let God speak to us, or we shall die." ²⁰Moses answered the people, "Do not be afraid, for God has come only to test you and put the fear of him upon you so you do not sin." ²¹So the people remained at a distance, while Moses approached the dark cloud where God was.

²² The LORD said to Moses: This is what you will say to the Israelites: You have seen for yourselves that I have spoken to you from heaven. ²³You shall not make alongside of me gods of silver, nor shall you make for yourselves gods of gold. ²⁴An altar of earth make for me, and sacrifice upon it your burnt offerings and communion sacrifices, your sheep and your oxen. In every place where I cause my name to be invoked I will come to you and bless you. ²⁵But if you make an altar of stone for me, do not build it of cut stone, for by putting a chisel to it you profane it. ²⁶You shall not ascend to my altar by steps, lest your nakedness be exposed.

The Gospel of Mark

John Mark, 64-70 AD

The earliest Christian histories tell us that the Gospel of Mark was written by a man named John Mark, who had been a travelling companion of Paul and later Peter's interpreter in Rome. On the basis of internal textual evidence, biblical scholars typically date the text to sometime around 70 A.D. This makes a good deal of sense. According to tradition, Peter died in the persecutions of Nero in the 60s AD, and Mark may have composed the gospel to preserve Peter's words and to console the Christian community in Rome, reeling from the shock of persecution.

For centuries, Christians thought that Mark was a shortened version of Matthew's gospel and that Matthew had been written first. This is why Matthew comes first in the New Testament. Modern scholars, pointing to the fact that Matthew and Luke share material from Mark and seemingly from another lost source (which scholars dub the Q-source), have argued that Mark wrote first, and then Matthew and Luke expanded on his work.

Scholars also debate the extent to which the Gospels represent what we would call history, with some claiming that almost none of it is reliable and others cherry-picking passages to mark out as authentic in order to recreate an historical Jesus in their own image. It is clear that Mark was certainly not writing in the genre that we call history. In the first place, he leaves out a lot of details that we would expect to find. In the second place, even the earliest testimonies admit that Mark did not write down events in chronological order. Finally, Mark was writing with an explicitly religious purpose, arranging his biography of Jesus to get across his central message: announcing the good news (gospel or Evangelion in Greek) that Jesus Christ was the son of God, who came to save us from our sins by his suffering and death on the cross.

This does not mean, however, that we should simply assume that nothing in the gospel actually happened, as some modern scholars assert with far more confidence than is warranted. If we assume that the author of Mark was relying on Peter or a Petrine tradition for his material, he was drawing on what historians would call a primary source and writing for an audience that must have included at least some surviving eye-witnesses. Moreover, the gospel shares many characteristics with the concerns of other ancient biographies, suggesting that both Mark and his audience were concerned with recording and preserving a version of what they had reason to believe actually happened. [95]

Chapter One

[1]The beginning of the gospel of Jesus Christ [the Son of God]. *The Preaching of John the Baptist.* [2] As it is written in Isaiah the prophet:

"Behold, I am sending my messenger ahead of you;
he will prepare your way.
[3] A voice of one crying out in the desert:
'Prepare the way of the Lord,
make straight his paths.'"

[4]John [the] Baptist appeared in the desert proclaiming a baptism of repentance for the forgiveness of sins. [5]People of the whole Judean countryside and all the inhabitants of Jerusalem were going out to

---

[95] Scripture texts in this work are taken from the *New American Bible, revised edition* © 2010, 1991, 1986, 1970 Confraternity of Christian Doctrine, Washington, D.C. and are used by permission of the copyright owner. All Rights Reserved. No part of the New American Bible may be reproduced in any form without permission in writing from the copyright owner.

him and were being baptized by him in the Jordan River as they acknowledged their sins. ⁶John was clothed in camel's hair, with a leather belt around his waist. He fed on locusts and wild honey. ⁷And this is what he proclaimed: "One mightier than I is coming after me. I am not worthy to stoop and loosen the thongs of his sandals. ⁸ I have baptized you with water; he will baptize you with the holy Spirit."

⁹ It happened in those days that Jesus came from Nazareth of Galilee and was baptized in the Jordan by John. ¹⁰On coming up out of the water he saw the heavens being torn open and the Spirit, like a dove, descending upon him. ¹¹ And a voice came from the heavens, "You are my beloved Son; with you I am well pleased."

¹²At once the Spirit drove him out into the desert, ¹³and he remained in the desert for forty days, tempted by Satan. He was among wild beasts, and the angels ministered to him.

¹⁴After John had been arrested, Jesus came to Galilee proclaiming the gospel of God: ¹⁵ "This is the time of fulfillment. The kingdom of God is at hand. Repent, and believe in the gospel."

¹⁶As he passed by the Sea of Galilee, he saw Simon and his brother Andrew casting their nets into the sea; they were fishermen. ¹⁷Jesus said to them, "Come after me, and I will make you fishers of men." ¹⁸Then they abandoned their nets and followed him. ¹⁹He walked along a little farther and saw James, the son of Zebedee, and his brother John. They too were in a boat mending their nets. ²⁰Then he called them. So they left their father Zebedee in the boat along with the hired men and followed him.

²¹Then they came to Capernaum, and on the sabbath he entered the synagogue and taught. ²² The people were astonished at his teaching, for he taught them as one having authority and not as the scribes. ²³ In their synagogue was a man with an unclean spirit; ²⁴ he cried out, "What have you to do with us, Jesus of Nazareth? Have you come to destroy us? I know who you are—the Holy One of God!" ²⁵Jesus rebuked him and said, "Quiet! Come out of him!" ²⁶The unclean spirit convulsed him and with a loud cry came out of him. ²⁷All were amazed and asked one another, "What is this? A new

teaching with authority. He commands even the unclean spirits and they obey him." ²⁸His fame spread everywhere throughout the whole region of Galilee.

²⁹ On leaving the synagogue he entered the house of Simon and Andrew with James and John. ³⁰Simon's mother-in-law lay sick with a fever. They immediately told him about her. ³¹He approached, grasped her hand, and helped her up. Then the fever left her and she waited on them.

³²When it was evening, after sunset, they brought to him all who were ill or possessed by demons. ³³The whole town was gathered at the door. ³⁴He cured many who were sick with various diseases, and he drove out many demons, not permitting them to speak because they knew him.

³⁵ Rising very early before dawn, he left and went off to a deserted place, where he prayed. ³⁶Simon and those who were with him pursued him ³⁷and on finding him said, "Everyone is looking for you." ³⁸He told them, "Let us go on to the nearby villages that I may preach there also. For this purpose have I come." ³⁹So he went into their synagogues, preaching and driving out demons throughout the whole of Galilee.

⁴⁰ A leper came to him [and kneeling down] begged him and said, "If you wish, you can make me clean." ⁴¹Moved with pity, he stretched out his hand, touched him, and said to him, "I do will it. Be made clean." ⁴²The leprosy left him immediately, and he was made clean. ⁴³Then, warning him sternly, he dismissed him at once. ⁴⁴Then he said to him, "See that you tell no one anything, but go, show yourself to the priest and offer for your cleansing what Moses prescribed; that will be proof for them." ⁴⁵The man went away and began to publicize the whole matter. He spread the report abroad so that it was impossible for Jesus to enter a town openly. He remained outside in deserted places, and people kept coming to him from everywhere.

Chapter Two

¹ When Jesus returned to Capernaum after some days, it became known that he was at home. ²Many gathered together so that there was no longer room for them, not even around the door, and he preached the word to them. ³They came bringing to him a paralytic carried by four men. ⁴Unable to get near Jesus because of the crowd, they opened up the roof above him. After they had broken through, they let down the mat on which the paralytic was lying. ⁵ When Jesus saw their faith, he said to the paralytic, "Child, your sins are forgiven." ⁶ Now some of the scribes were sitting there asking themselves, ⁷"Why does this man speak that way? He is blaspheming. Who but God alone can forgive sins?" ⁸Jesus immediately knew in his mind what they were thinking to themselves, so he said, "Why are you thinking such things in your hearts? ⁹Which is easier, to say to the paralytic, 'Your sins are forgiven,' or to say, 'Rise, pick up your mat and walk'? ¹⁰ But that you may know that the Son of Man has authority to forgive sins on earth"— ¹¹he said to the paralytic, "I say to you, rise, pick up your mat, and go home." ¹²He rose, picked up his mat at once, and went away in the sight of everyone. They were all astounded and glorified God, saying, "We have never seen anything like this."

¹³ Once again he went out along the sea. All the crowd came to him and he taught them. ¹⁴ As he passed by, he saw Levi, son of Alphaeus, sitting at the customs post. He said to him, "Follow me." And he got up and followed him. ¹⁵While he was at table in his house, many tax collectors and sinners sat with Jesus and his disciples; for there were many who followed him. ¹⁶ Some scribes who were Pharisees saw that he was eating with sinners and tax collectors and said to his disciples, "Why does he eat with tax collectors and sinners?" ¹⁷Jesus heard this and said to them [that], "Those who are well do not need a physician, but the sick do. I did not come to call the righteous but sinners."

¹⁸The disciples of John and of the Pharisees were accustomed to fast. People came to him and objected, "Why do the disciples of John and the disciples of the Pharisees fast, but your disciples do not fast?"

¹⁹Jesus answered them, "Can the wedding guests fast while the bridegroom is with them? As long as they have the bridegroom with them they cannot fast. ²⁰But the days will come when the bridegroom is taken away from them, and then they will fast on that day. ²¹No one sews a piece of unshrunken cloth on an old cloak. If he does, its fullness pulls away, the new from the old, and the tear gets worse. ²²Likewise, no one pours new wine into old wineskins. Otherwise, the wine will burst the skins, and both the wine and the skins are ruined. Rather, new wine is poured into fresh wineskins."

²³As he was passing through a field of grain on the sabbath, his disciples began to make a path while picking the heads of grain. ²⁴At this the Pharisees said to him, "Look, why are they doing what is unlawful on the sabbath?" ²⁵He said to them, "Have you never read what David did when he was in need and he and his companions were hungry? ²⁶How he went into the house of God when Abiathar was high priest and ate the bread of offering that only the priests could lawfully eat, and shared it with his companions?" ²⁷Then he said to them, "The sabbath was made for man, not man for the sabbath. ²⁸ That is why the Son of Man is lord even of the sabbath."

Chapter Three

¹ Again he entered the synagogue. There was a man there who had a withered hand. ²They watched him closely to see if he would cure him on the sabbath so that they might accuse him. ³He said to the man with the withered hand, "Come up here before us." ⁴Then he said to them, "Is it lawful to do good on the sabbath rather than to do evil, to save life rather than to destroy it?" But they remained silent. ⁵Looking around at them with anger and grieved at their hardness of heart, he said to the man, "Stretch out your hand." He stretched it out and his hand was restored. ⁶ The Pharisees went out and immediately took counsel with the Herodians against him to put him to death.

⁷ Jesus withdrew toward the sea with his disciples. A large number of people [followed] from Galilee and from Judea. ⁸Hearing

what he was doing, a large number of people came to him also from Jerusalem, from Idumea, from beyond the Jordan, and from the neighborhood of Tyre and Sidon. ⁹He told his disciples to have a boat ready for him because of the crowd, so that they would not crush him. ¹⁰He had cured many and, as a result, those who had diseases were pressing upon him to touch him. ¹¹ And whenever unclean spirits saw him they would fall down before him and shout, "You are the Son of God." ¹²He warned them sternly not to make him known.

¹³ He went up the mountain and summoned those whom he wanted and they came to him. ¹⁴ He appointed twelve [whom he also named apostles] that they might be with him and he might send them forth to preach ¹⁵and to have authority to drive out demons: ¹⁶ [he appointed the twelve:] Simon, whom he named Peter; ¹⁷James, son of Zebedee, and John the brother of James, whom he named Boanerges, that is, sons of thunder; ¹⁸Andrew, Philip, Bartholomew, Matthew, Thomas, James the son of Alphaeus; Thaddeus, Simon the Cananean, ¹⁹and Judas Iscariot who betrayed him.

²⁰He came home. Again [the] crowd gathered, making it impossible for them even to eat. ²¹When his relatives heard of this they set out to seize him, for they said, "He is out of his mind." ²²The scribes who had come from Jerusalem said, "He is possessed by Beelzebul," and "By the prince of demons he drives out demons."

²³Summoning them, he began to speak to them in parables, "How can Satan drive out Satan? ²⁴If a kingdom is divided against itself, that kingdom cannot stand. ²⁵And if a house is divided against itself, that house will not be able to stand. ²⁶And if Satan has risen up against himself and is divided, he cannot stand; that is the end of him. ²⁷But no one can enter a strong man's house to plunder his property unless he first ties up the strong man. Then he can plunder his house. ²⁸Amen, I say to you, all sins and all blasphemies that people utter will be forgiven them. ²⁹But whoever blasphemes against the holy Spirit will never have forgiveness, but is guilty of an everlasting sin." ³⁰For they had said, "He has an unclean spirit."

³¹ His mother and his brothers arrived. Standing outside they sent word to him and called him. ³²A crowd seated around him told

him, "Your mother and your brothers [and your sisters] are outside asking for you." ³³But he said to them in reply, "Who are my mother and [my] brothers?" ³⁴And looking around at those seated in the circle he said, "Here are my mother and my brothers. ³⁵[For] whoever does the will of God is my brother and sister and mother."

Chapter Four

¹ On another occasion he began to teach by the sea. A very large crowd gathered around him so that he got into a boat on the sea and sat down. And the whole crowd was beside the sea on land. ²And he taught them at length in parables, and in the course of his instruction he said to them, ³ "Hear this! A sower went out to sow. ⁴And as he sowed, some seed fell on the path, and the birds came and ate it up. ⁵Other seed fell on rocky ground where it had little soil. It sprang up at once because the soil was not deep. ⁶And when the sun rose, it was scorched and it withered for lack of roots. ⁷Some seed fell among thorns, and the thorns grew up and choked it and it produced no grain. ⁸And some seed fell on rich soil and produced fruit. It came up and grew and yielded thirty, sixty, and a hundredfold." ⁹He added, "Whoever has ears to hear ought to hear."

¹⁰And when he was alone, those present along with the Twelve questioned him about the parables. ¹¹ He answered them, "The mystery of the kingdom of God has been granted to you. But to those outside everything comes in parables, ¹²so that

'they may look and see but not perceive,
and hear and listen but not understand,
in order that they may not be converted and be forgiven.'"

¹³ Jesus said to them, "Do you not understand this parable? Then how will you understand any of the parables? ¹⁴The sower sows the word. ¹⁵These are the ones on the path where the word is sown. As soon as they hear, Satan comes at once and takes away the word sown in them. ¹⁶And these are the ones sown on rocky ground who,

when they hear the word, receive it at once with joy. [17]But they have no root; they last only for a time. Then when tribulation or persecution comes because of the word, they quickly fall away. [18]Those sown among thorns are another sort. They are the people who hear the word, [19]but worldly anxiety, the lure of riches, and the craving for other things intrude and choke the word, and it bears no fruit. [20]But those sown on rich soil are the ones who hear the word and accept it and bear fruit thirty and sixty and a hundredfold."

[21]He said to them, "Is a lamp brought in to be placed under a bushel basket or under a bed, and not to be placed on a lampstand? [22]For there is nothing hidden except to be made visible; nothing is secret except to come to light. [23]Anyone who has ears to hear ought to hear." [24]He also told them, "Take care what you hear. The measure with which you measure will be measured out to you, and still more will be given to you. [25]To the one who has, more will be given; from the one who has not, even what he has will be taken away."

[26]He said, "This is how it is with the kingdom of God; it is as if a man were to scatter seed on the land [27]and would sleep and rise night and day and the seed would sprout and grow, he knows not how. [28]Of its own accord the land yields fruit, first the blade, then the ear, then the full grain in the ear. [29]And when the grain is ripe, he wields the sickle at once, for the harvest has come."

[30] He said, "To what shall we compare the kingdom of God, or what parable can we use for it? [31]It is like a mustard seed that, when it is sown in the ground, is the smallest of all the seeds on the earth. [32] But once it is sown, it springs up and becomes the largest of plants and puts forth large branches, so that the birds of the sky can dwell in its shade." [33]With many such parables he spoke the word to them as they were able to understand it. [34]Without parables he did not speak to them, but to his own disciples he explained everything in private.

[35]On that day, as evening drew on, he said to them, "Let us cross to the other side." [36]Leaving the crowd, they took him with them in the boat just as he was. And other boats were with him. [37]A violent squall came up and waves were breaking over the boat, so that it was

already filling up. ³⁸Jesus was in the stern, asleep on a cushion. They woke him and said to him, "Teacher, do you not care that we are perishing?" ³⁹He woke up, rebuked the wind, and said to the sea, "Quiet! Be still!" The wind ceased and there was great calm. ⁴⁰Then he asked them, "Why are you terrified? Do you not yet have faith?" ⁴¹ They were filled with great awe and said to one another, "Who then is this whom even wind and sea obey?"

Chapter Five

¹ They came to the other side of the sea, to the territory of the Gerasenes. ²When he got out of the boat, at once a man from the tombs who had an unclean spirit met him. ³The man had been dwelling among the tombs, and no one could restrain him any longer, even with a chain. ⁴In fact, he had frequently been bound with shackles and chains, but the chains had been pulled apart by him and the shackles smashed, and no one was strong enough to subdue him. ⁵Night and day among the tombs and on the hillsides he was always crying out and bruising himself with stones. ⁶Catching sight of Jesus from a distance, he ran up and prostrated himself before him, ⁷crying out in a loud voice, "What have you to do with me, Jesus, Son of the Most High God? I adjure you by God, do not torment me!" ⁸(He had been saying to him, "Unclean spirit, come out of the man!") ⁹ He asked him, "What is your name?" He replied, "Legion is my name. There are many of us." ¹⁰And he pleaded earnestly with him not to drive them away from that territory.

¹¹Now a large herd of swine was feeding there on the hillside. ¹²And they pleaded with him, "Send us into the swine. Let us enter them." ¹³And he let them, and the unclean spirits came out and entered the swine. The herd of about two thousand rushed down a steep bank into the sea, where they were drowned. ¹⁴The swineherds ran away and reported the incident in the town and throughout the countryside. And people came out to see what had happened. ¹⁵As they approached Jesus, they caught sight of the man who had been possessed by Legion, sitting there clothed and in his right mind. And

they were seized with fear. [16]Those who witnessed the incident explained to them what had happened to the possessed man and to the swine. [17]Then they began to beg him to leave their district. [18]As he was getting into the boat, the man who had been possessed pleaded to remain with him. [19]But he would not permit him but told him instead, "Go home to your family and announce to them all that the Lord in his pity has done for you." [20]Then the man went off and began to proclaim in the Decapolis what Jesus had done for him; and all were amazed.

[21]When Jesus had crossed again [in the boat] to the other side, a large crowd gathered around him, and he stayed close to the sea. [22]One of the synagogue officials, named Jairus, came forward. Seeing him he fell at his feet [23]and pleaded earnestly with him, saying, "My daughter is at the point of death. Please, come lay your hands on her that she may get well and live." [24]He went off with him, and a large crowd followed him and pressed upon him.

[25]There was a woman afflicted with hemorrhages for twelve years. [26]She had suffered greatly at the hands of many doctors and had spent all that she had. Yet she was not helped but only grew worse. [27]She had heard about Jesus and came up behind him in the crowd and touched his cloak. [28] She said, "If I but touch his clothes, I shall be cured." [29]Immediately her flow of blood dried up. She felt in her body that she was healed of her affliction. [30]Jesus, aware at once that power had gone out from him, turned around in the crowd and asked, "Who has touched my clothes?" [31]But his disciples said to him, "You see how the crowd is pressing upon you, and yet you ask, 'Who touched me?'" [32]And he looked around to see who had done it. [33]The woman, realizing what had happened to her, approached in fear and trembling. She fell down before Jesus and told him the whole truth. [34]He said to her, "Daughter, your faith has saved you. Go in peace and be cured of your affliction."

[35]While he was still speaking, people from the synagogue official's house arrived and said, "Your daughter has died; why trouble the teacher any longer?" [36]Disregarding the message that was reported, Jesus said to the synagogue official, "Do not be afraid; just

have faith." ³⁷He did not allow anyone to accompany him inside except Peter, James, and John, the brother of James. ³⁸When they arrived at the house of the synagogue official, he caught sight of a commotion, people weeping and wailing loudly. ³⁹ So he went in and said to them, "Why this commotion and weeping? The child is not dead but asleep." ⁴⁰And they ridiculed him. Then he put them all out. He took along the child's father and mother and those who were with him and entered the room where the child was. ⁴¹ He took the child by the hand and said to her, *"Talitha koum,"* which means, "Little girl, I say to you, arise!" ⁴²The girl, a child of twelve, arose immediately and walked around. [At that] they were utterly astounded. ⁴³He gave strict orders that no one should know this and said that she should be given something to eat.

Chapter Six

¹ He departed from there and came to his native place, accompanied by his disciples. ² When the sabbath came he began to teach in the synagogue, and many who heard him were astonished. They said, "Where did this man get all this? What kind of wisdom has been given him? What mighty deeds are wrought by his hands! ³ Is he not the carpenter, the son of Mary, and the brother of James and Joses and Judas and Simon? And are not his sisters here with us?" And they took offense at him. ⁴ Jesus said to them, "A prophet is not without honor except in his native place and among his own kin and in his own house." ⁵So he was not able to perform any mighty deed there, apart from curing a few sick people by laying his hands on them. ⁶He was amazed at their lack of faith.

He went around to the villages in the vicinity teaching. ⁷ He summoned the Twelve and began to send them out two by two and gave them authority over unclean spirits. ⁸ He instructed them to take nothing for the journey but a walking stick—no food, no sack, no money in their belts. ⁹They were, however, to wear sandals but not a second tunic. ¹⁰ He said to them, "Wherever you enter a house, stay there until you leave from there. ¹¹Whatever place does not welcome you or listen to you, leave there and shake the dust off your feet in testimony against them." [12]So they went off and preached repentance. [13] They drove out many demons, and they anointed with oil many who were sick and cured them.

[14]King Herod heard about it, for his fame had become widespread, and people were saying, "John the Baptist has been raised from the dead; that is why mighty powers are at work in him." [15]Others were saying, "He is Elijah"; still others, "He is a prophet like any of the prophets." [16]But when Herod learned of it, he said, "It is John whom I beheaded. He has been raised up."

[17]Herod was the one who had John arrested and bound in prison on account of Herodias, the wife of his brother Philip, whom he had married. [18]John had said to Herod, "It is not lawful for you to have your brother's wife." [19]Herodias harbored a grudge against him and wanted to kill him but was unable to do so. [20]Herod feared John, knowing him to be a righteous and holy man, and kept him in custody. When he heard him speak he was very much perplexed, yet he liked to listen to him. [21]She had an opportunity one day when Herod, on his birthday, gave a banquet for his courtiers, his military officers, and the leading men of Galilee. [22]Herodias's own daughter came in and performed a dance that delighted Herod and his guests. The king said to the girl, "Ask of me whatever you wish and I will grant it to you." [23]He even swore [many things] to her, "I will grant you whatever you ask of me, even to half of my kingdom." [24]She went out and said to her mother, "What shall I ask for?" She replied, "The head of John the Baptist." [25]The girl hurried back to the king's presence and made her request, "I want you to give me at once on a platter the head of John the Baptist." [26]The king was deeply distressed, but because of his oaths and the guests he did not wish to break his word to her. [27] So he promptly dispatched an executioner with orders to bring back his head. He went off and beheaded him in the prison. [28]He brought in the head on a platter and gave it to the girl. The girl in turn gave it to her mother. [29]When his disciples heard about it, they came and took his body and laid it in a tomb.

³⁰The apostles gathered together with Jesus and reported all they had done and taught. ³¹ He said to them, "Come away by yourselves to a deserted place and rest a while." People were coming and going in great numbers, and they had no opportunity even to eat. ³²So they went off in the boat by themselves to a deserted place. ³³People saw them leaving and many came to know about it. They hastened there on foot from all the towns and arrived at the place before them.

³⁴When he disembarked and saw the vast crowd, his heart was moved with pity for them, for they were like sheep without a shepherd; and he began to teach them many things. ³⁵ By now it was already late and his disciples approached him and said, "This is a deserted place and it is already very late. ³⁶Dismiss them so that they can go to the surrounding farms and villages and buy themselves something to eat." ³⁷He said to them in reply, "Give them some food yourselves." But they said to him, "Are we to buy two hundred days' wages worth of food and give it to them to eat?" ³⁸He asked them, "How many loaves do you have? Go and see." And when they had found out they said, "Five loaves and two fish." ³⁹So he gave orders to have them sit down in groups on the green grass. ⁴⁰ The people took their places in rows by hundreds and by fifties. ⁴¹Then, taking the five loaves and the two fish and looking up to heaven, he said the blessing, broke the loaves, and gave them to [his] disciples to set before the people; he also divided the two fish among them all. ⁴²They all ate and were satisfied. ⁴³And they picked up twelve wicker baskets full of fragments and what was left of the fish. ⁴⁴Those who ate [of the loaves] were five thousand men.

⁴⁵Then he made his disciples get into the boat and precede him to the other side toward Bethsaida, while he dismissed the crowd. ⁴⁶ And when he had taken leave of them, he went off to the mountain to pray. ⁴⁷When it was evening, the boat was far out on the sea and he was alone on shore. ⁴⁸Then he saw that they were tossed about while rowing, for the wind was against them. About the fourth watch of the night, he came toward them walking on the sea. He meant to pass by them. ⁴⁹But when they saw him walking on the sea, they thought it was a ghost and cried out. ⁵⁰ They had all seen him and

were terrified. But at once he spoke with them, "Take courage, it is I, do not be afraid!" [51]He got into the boat with them and the wind died down. They were [completely] astounded. [52]They had not understood the incident of the loaves. On the contrary, their hearts were hardened.

[53]After making the crossing, they came to land at Gennesaret and tied up there. [54]As they were leaving the boat, people immediately recognized him. [55]They scurried about the surrounding country and began to bring in the sick on mats to wherever they heard he was. [56]Whatever villages or towns or countryside he entered, they laid the sick in the marketplaces and begged him that they might touch only the tassel on his cloak; and as many as touched it were healed.

Chapter Seven

[1]Now when the Pharisees with some scribes who had come from Jerusalem gathered around him, [2]they observed that some of his disciples ate their meals with unclean, that is, unwashed, hands. [3](For the Pharisees and, in fact, all Jews, do not eat without carefully washing their hands, keeping the tradition of the elders. [4]And on coming from the marketplace they do not eat without purifying themselves. And there are many other things that they have traditionally observed, the purification of cups and jugs and kettles [and beds].) [5]So the Pharisees and scribes questioned him, "Why do your disciples not follow the tradition of the elders but instead eat a meal with unclean hands?" [6]He responded,

"Well did Isaiah prophesy about you hypocrites, as it is written:
'This people honors me with their lips,
but their hearts are far from me;
[7]In vain do they worship me,
teaching as doctrines human precepts.'

⁸You disregard God's commandment but cling to human tradition." ⁹He went on to say, "How well you have set aside the commandment of God in order to uphold your tradition! ¹⁰For Moses said, 'Honor your father and your mother,' and 'Whoever curses father or mother shall die.' ¹¹Yet you say, 'If a person says to father or mother, "Any support you might have had from me is *qorban*"' (meaning, dedicated to God), ¹²you allow him to do nothing more for his father or mother. ¹³You nullify the word of God in favor of your tradition that you have handed on. And you do many such things."

¹⁴ He summoned the crowd again and said to them, "Hear me, all of you, and understand. ¹⁵Nothing that enters one from outside can defile that person; but the things that come out from within are what defile." ¹⁶

¹⁷ When he got home away from the crowd his disciples questioned him about the parable. ¹⁸He said to them, "Are even you likewise without understanding? Do you not realize that everything that goes into a person from outside cannot defile, ¹⁹ since it enters not the heart but the stomach and passes out into the latrine?" (Thus he declared all foods clean.) ²⁰"But what comes out of a person, that is what defiles. ²¹ From within people, from their hearts, come evil thoughts, unchastity, theft, murder, ²²adultery, greed, malice, deceit, licentiousness, envy, blasphemy, arrogance, folly. ²³All these evils come from within and they defile."

²⁴From that place he went off to the district of Tyre. He entered a house and wanted no one to know about it, but he could not escape notice. ²⁵Soon a woman whose daughter had an unclean spirit heard about him. She came and fell at his feet. ²⁶The woman was a Greek, a Syrophoenician by birth, and she begged him to drive the demon out of her daughter. ²⁷He said to her, "Let the children be fed first. For it is not right to take the food of the children and throw it to the dogs." ²⁸She replied and said to him, "Lord, even the dogs under the table eat the children's scraps." ²⁹Then he said to her, "For saying this, you may go. The demon has gone out of your daughter." ³⁰When the woman went home, she found the child lying in bed and the demon gone.

³¹ Again he left the district of Tyre and went by way of Sidon to the Sea of Galilee, into the district of the Decapolis. ³²And people brought to him a deaf man who had a speech impediment and begged him to lay his hand on him. ³³He took him off by himself away from the crowd. He put his finger into the man's ears and, spitting, touched his tongue; ³⁴then he looked up to heaven and groaned, and said to him, "*Ephphatha!*" (that is, "Be opened!") ³⁵And [immediately] the man's ears were opened, his speech impediment was removed, and he spoke plainly. ³⁶ He ordered them not to tell anyone. But the more he ordered them not to, the more they proclaimed it. ³⁷They were exceedingly astonished and they said, "He has done all things well. He makes the deaf hear and [the] mute speak."

Chapter Eight

¹In those days when there again was a great crowd without anything to eat, he summoned the disciples and said, ²"My heart is moved with pity for the crowd, because they have been with me now for three days and have nothing to eat. ³If I send them away hungry to their homes, they will collapse on the way, and some of them have come a great distance." ⁴His disciples answered him, "Where can anyone get enough bread to satisfy them here in this deserted place?" ⁵Still he asked them, "How many loaves do you have?" "Seven," they replied. ⁶ He ordered the crowd to sit down on the ground. Then, taking the seven loaves he gave thanks, broke them, and gave them to his disciples to distribute, and they distributed them to the crowd. ⁷They also had a few fish. He said the blessing over them and ordered them distributed also. ⁸They ate and were satisfied. They picked up the fragments left over—seven baskets. ⁹There were about four thousand people.

He dismissed them ¹⁰and got into the boat with his disciples and came to the region of Dalmanutha.

¹¹The Pharisees came forward and began to argue with him, seeking from him a sign from heaven to test him. ¹²He sighed from the depth of his spirit and said, "Why does this generation seek a

sign? Amen, I say to you, no sign will be given to this generation." ¹³Then he left them, got into the boat again, and went off to the other shore.

¹⁴They had forgotten to bring bread, and they had only one loaf with them in the boat. ¹⁵ He enjoined them, "Watch out, guard against the leaven of the Pharisees and the leaven of Herod." ¹⁶They concluded among themselves that it was because they had no bread. ¹⁷When he became aware of this he said to them, "Why do you conclude that it is because you have no bread? Do you not yet understand or comprehend? Are your hearts hardened? ¹⁸Do you have eyes and not see, ears and not hear? And do you not remember, ¹⁹when I broke the five loaves for the five thousand, how many wicker baskets full of fragments you picked up?" They answered him, "Twelve." ²⁰"When I broke the seven loaves for the four thousand, how many full baskets of fragments did you pick up?" They answered [him], "Seven." ²¹He said to them, "Do you still not understand?"

²²When they arrived at Bethsaida, they brought to him a blind man and begged him to touch him. ²³He took the blind man by the hand and led him outside the village. Putting spittle on his eyes he laid his hands on him and asked, "Do you see anything?" ²⁴Looking up he replied, "I see people looking like trees and walking." ²⁵Then he laid hands on his eyes a second time and he saw clearly; his sight was restored and he could see everything distinctly. ²⁶Then he sent him home and said, "Do not even go into the village."

²⁷Now Jesus and his disciples set out for the villages of Caesarea Philippi. Along the way he asked his disciples, "Who do people say that I am?" ²⁸They said in reply, "John the Baptist, others Elijah, still others one of the prophets." ²⁹And he asked them, "But who do you say that I am?" Peter said to him in reply, "You are the Messiah." ³⁰Then he warned them not to tell anyone about him.

³¹He began to teach them that the Son of Man must suffer greatly and be rejected by the elders, the chief priests, and the scribes, and be killed, and rise after three days. ³²He spoke this openly. Then Peter took him aside and began to rebuke him. ³³At this he turned around

and, looking at his disciples, rebuked Peter and said, "Get behind me, Satan. You are thinking not as God does, but as human beings do."

³⁴He summoned the crowd with his disciples and said to them, "Whoever wishes to come after me must deny himself, take up his cross, and follow me. ³⁵For whoever wishes to save his life will lose it, but whoever loses his life for my sake and that of the gospel will save it. ³⁶What profit is there for one to gain the whole world and forfeit his life? ³⁷What could one give in exchange for his life? ³⁸Whoever is ashamed of me and of my words in this faithless and sinful generation, the Son of Man will be ashamed of when he comes in his Father's glory with the holy angels."

Chapter Nine

¹ He also said to them, "Amen, I say to you, there are some standing here who will not taste death until they see that the kingdom of God has come in power."

²After six days Jesus took Peter, James, and John and led them up a high mountain apart by themselves. And he was transfigured before them, ³and his clothes became dazzling white, such as no fuller on earth could bleach them. ⁴Then Elijah appeared to them along with Moses, and they were conversing with Jesus. ⁵ Then Peter said to Jesus in reply, "Rabbi, it is good that we are here! Let us make three tents: one for you, one for Moses, and one for Elijah." ⁶He hardly knew what to say, they were so terrified. ⁷Then a cloud came, casting a shadow over them; then from the cloud came a voice, "This is my beloved Son. Listen to him." ⁸Suddenly, looking around, they no longer saw anyone but Jesus alone with them.

⁹As they were coming down from the mountain, he charged them not to relate what they had seen to anyone, except when the Son of Man had risen from the dead. ¹⁰So they kept the matter to themselves, questioning what rising from the dead meant. ¹¹ Then they asked him, "Why do the scribes say that Elijah must come first?" ¹²He told them, "Elijah will indeed come first and restore all things, yet how is it written regarding the Son of Man that he must suffer greatly and

be treated with contempt? [13]But I tell you that Elijah has come and they did to him whatever they pleased, as it is written of him."

[14]When they came to the disciples, they saw a large crowd around them and scribes arguing with them. [15]Immediately on seeing him, the whole crowd was utterly amazed. They ran up to him and greeted him. [16]He asked them, "What are you arguing about with them?" [17]Someone from the crowd answered him, "Teacher, I have brought to you my son possessed by a mute spirit. [18]Wherever it seizes him, it throws him down; he foams at the mouth, grinds his teeth, and becomes rigid. I asked your disciples to drive it out, but they were unable to do so." [19]He said to them in reply, "O faithless generation, how long will I be with you? How long will I endure you? Bring him to me." [20]They brought the boy to him. And when he saw him, the spirit immediately threw the boy into convulsions. As he fell to the ground, he began to roll around and foam at the mouth. [21]Then he questioned his father, "How long has this been happening to him?" He replied, "Since childhood. [22]It has often thrown him into fire and into water to kill him. But if you can do anything, have compassion on us and help us." [23]Jesus said to him, "'If you can!' Everything is possible to one who has faith." [24]Then the boy's father cried out, "I do believe, help my unbelief!" [25]Jesus, on seeing a crowd rapidly gathering, rebuked the unclean spirit and said to it, "Mute and deaf spirit, I command you: come out of him and never enter him again!" [26]Shouting and throwing the boy into convulsions, it came out. He became like a corpse, which caused many to say, "He is dead!" [27]But Jesus took him by the hand, raised him, and he stood up. [28]When he entered the house, his disciples asked him in private, "Why could we not drive it out?" [29] He said to them, "This kind can only come out through prayer."

[30] They left from there and began a journey through Galilee, but he did not wish anyone to know about it. [31]He was teaching his disciples and telling them, "The Son of Man is to be handed over to men and they will kill him, and three days after his death he will rise." [32]But they did not understand the saying, and they were afraid to question him.

³³They came to Capernaum and, once inside the house, he began to ask them, "What were you arguing about on the way?" ³⁴But they remained silent. They had been discussing among themselves on the way who was the greatest. ³⁵Then he sat down, called the Twelve, and said to them, "If anyone wishes to be first, he shall be the last of all and the servant of all." ³⁶Taking a child he placed it in their midst, and putting his arms around it he said to them, ³⁷"Whoever receives one child such as this in my name, receives me; and whoever receives me, receives not me but the One who sent me."

³⁸John said to him, "Teacher, we saw someone driving out demons in your name, and we tried to prevent him because he does not follow us." ³⁹Jesus replied, "Do not prevent him. There is no one who performs a mighty deed in my name who can at the same time speak ill of me. ⁴⁰For whoever is not against us is for us. ⁴¹Anyone who gives you a cup of water to drink because you belong to Christ, amen, I say to you, will surely not lose his reward.

⁴²"Whoever causes one of these little ones who believe [in me] to sin, it would be better for him if a great millstone were put around his neck and he were thrown into the sea. ⁴³If your hand causes you to sin, cut it off. It is better for you to enter into life maimed than with two hands to go into Gehenna, into the unquenchable fire. ⁴⁴ ⁴⁵And if your foot causes you to sin, cut it off. It is better for you to enter into life crippled than with two feet to be thrown into Gehenna. ⁴⁷And if your eye causes you to sin, pluck it out. Better for you to enter into the kingdom of God with one eye than with two eyes to be thrown into Gehenna, ⁴⁸where 'their worm does not die, and the fire is not quenched.'

⁴⁹"Everyone will be salted with fire. ⁵⁰Salt is good, but if salt becomes insipid, with what will you restore its flavor? Keep salt in yourselves and you will have peace with one another."

Chapter Ten

¹He set out from there and went into the district of Judea [and] across the Jordan. Again crowds gathered around him and, as was

his custom, he again taught them. 2 The Pharisees approached and asked, "Is it lawful for a husband to divorce his wife?" They were testing him. ³He said to them in reply, "What did Moses command you?" ⁴They replied, "Moses permitted him to write a bill of divorce and dismiss her." ⁵But Jesus told them, "Because of the hardness of your hearts he wrote you this commandment. ⁶But from the beginning of creation, 'God made them male and female. ⁷For this reason a man shall leave his father and mother [and be joined to his wife], ⁸and the two shall become one flesh.' So they are no longer two but one flesh. ⁹Therefore what God has joined together, no human being must separate." ¹⁰In the house the disciples again questioned him about this. ¹¹ He said to them, "Whoever divorces his wife and marries another commits adultery against her; ¹²and if she divorces her husband and marries another, she commits adultery."

¹³And people were bringing children to him that he might touch them, but the disciples rebuked them. ¹⁴When Jesus saw this he became indignant and said to them, "Let the children come to me; do not prevent them, for the kingdom of God belongs to such as these. ¹⁵Amen, I say to you, whoever does not accept the kingdom of God like a child will not enter it." ¹⁶Then he embraced them and blessed them, placing his hands on them.

¹⁷As he was setting out on a journey, a man ran up, knelt down before him, and asked, "Good teacher, what must I do to inherit eternal life?" ¹⁸Jesus answered him, "Why do you call me good? No one is good but God alone. ¹⁹You know the commandments: 'You shall not kill; you shall not commit adultery; you shall not steal; you shall not bear false witness; you shall not defraud; honor your father and your mother.'" ²⁰He replied and said to him, "Teacher, all of these I have observed from my youth."

²¹Jesus, looking at him, loved him and said to him, "You are lacking in one thing. Go, sell what you have, and give to [the] poor and you will have treasure in heaven; then come, follow me." ²²At that statement his face fell, and he went away sad, for he had many possessions.

²³Jesus looked around and said to his disciples, "How hard it is for those who have wealth to enter the kingdom of God!" ²⁴The disciples were amazed at his words. So Jesus again said to them in reply, "Children, how hard it is to enter the kingdom of God! ²⁵It is easier for a camel to pass through [the] eye of [a] needle than for one who is rich to enter the kingdom of God." ²⁶They were exceedingly astonished and said among themselves, "Then who can be saved?" ²⁷Jesus looked at them and said, "For human beings it is impossible, but not for God. All things are possible for God." ²⁸Peter began to say to him, "We have given up everything and followed you." ²⁹Jesus said, "Amen, I say to you, there is no one who has given up house or brothers or sisters or mother or father or children or lands for my sake and for the sake of the gospel ³⁰who will not receive a hundred times more now in this present age: houses and brothers and sisters and mothers and children and lands, with persecutions, and eternal life in the age to come. ³¹But many that are first will be last, and [the] last will be first."

³²They were on the way, going up to Jerusalem, and Jesus went ahead of them. They were amazed, and those who followed were afraid. Taking the Twelve aside again, he began to tell them what was going to happen to him. ³³"Behold, we are going up to Jerusalem, and the Son of Man will be handed over to the chief priests and the scribes, and they will condemn him to death and hand him over to the Gentiles ³⁴who will mock him, spit upon him, scourge him, and put him to death, but after three days he will rise."

³⁵Then James and John, the sons of Zebedee, came to him and said to him, "Teacher, we want you to do for us whatever we ask of you." ³⁶He replied, "What do you wish [me] to do for you?" ³⁷They answered him, "Grant that in your glory we may sit one at your right and the other at your left." ³⁸ Jesus said to them, "You do not know what you are asking. Can you drink the cup that I drink or be baptized with the baptism with which I am baptized?" ³⁹They said to him, "We can." Jesus said to them, "The cup that I drink, you will drink, and with the baptism with which I am baptized, you will be baptized; ⁴⁰but to sit at my right or at my left is not mine to give but

is for those for whom it has been prepared." ⁴¹When the ten heard this, they became indignant at James and John. ⁴² Jesus summoned them and said to them, "You know that those who are recognized as rulers over the Gentiles lord it over them, and their great ones make their authority over them felt. ⁴³But it shall not be so among you. Rather, whoever wishes to be great among you will be your servant; ⁴⁴whoever wishes to be first among you will be the slave of all. ⁴⁵For the Son of Man did not come to be served but to serve and to give his life as a ransom for many."

⁴⁶They came to Jericho. And as he was leaving Jericho with his disciples and a sizable crowd, Bartimaeus, a blind man, the son of Timaeus, sat by the roadside begging. ⁴⁷On hearing that it was Jesus of Nazareth, he began to cry out and say, "Jesus, son of David, have pity on me." ⁴⁸And many rebuked him, telling him to be silent. But he kept calling out all the more, "Son of David, have pity on me." ⁴⁹Jesus stopped and said, "Call him." So they called the blind man, saying to him, "Take courage; get up, he is calling you." ⁵⁰He threw aside his cloak, sprang up, and came to Jesus. ⁵¹Jesus said to him in reply, "What do you want me to do for you?" The blind man replied to him, "Master, I want to see." ⁵²Jesus told him, "Go your way; your faith has saved you." Immediately he received his sight and followed him on the way.

Chapter Eleven

¹When they drew near to Jerusalem, to Bethphage and Bethany at the Mount of Olives, he sent two of his disciples ²and said to them, "Go into the village opposite you, and immediately on entering it, you will find a colt tethered on which no one has ever sat. Untie it and bring it here. ³If anyone should say to you, 'Why are you doing this?' reply, 'The Master has need of it and will send it back here at once.'" ⁴So they went off and found a colt tethered at a gate outside on the street, and they untied it. ⁵Some of the bystanders said to them, "What are you doing, untying the colt?" ⁶They answered them just as Jesus had told them to, and they permitted them to do it. ⁷So they

brought the colt to Jesus and put their cloaks over it. And he sat on it. [8]Many people spread their cloaks on the road, and others spread leafy branches that they had cut from the fields. [9]Those preceding him as well as those following kept crying out:

> "Hosanna!
> Blessed is he who comes in the name of the Lord!
> [10]Blessed is the kingdom of our father David that is to come!
> Hosanna in the highest!"

[11]He entered Jerusalem and went into the temple area. He looked around at everything and, since it was already late, went out to Bethany with the Twelve.

[12]The next day as they were leaving Bethany he was hungry. [13]Seeing from a distance a fig tree in leaf, he went over to see if he could find anything on it. When he reached it he found nothing but leaves; it was not the time for figs. [14]And he said to it in reply, "May no one ever eat of your fruit again!" And his disciples heard it.

[15]They came to Jerusalem, and on entering the temple area he began to drive out those selling and buying there. He overturned the tables of the money changers and the seats of those who were selling doves. [16]He did not permit anyone to carry anything through the temple area. [17]Then he taught them saying, "Is it not written:

> 'My house shall be called a house of prayer for all peoples'?
> But you have made it a den of thieves."

[18]The chief priests and the scribes came to hear of it and were seeking a way to put him to death, yet they feared him because the whole crowd was astonished at his teaching. [19]When evening came, they went out of the city.

[20]Early in the morning, as they were walking along, they saw the fig tree withered to its roots. [21]Peter remembered and said to him, "Rabbi, look! The fig tree that you cursed has withered." [22]Jesus said to them in reply, "Have faith in God. [23]Amen, I say to you, whoever

says to this mountain, 'Be lifted up and thrown into the sea,' and does not doubt in his heart but believes that what he says will happen, it shall be done for him. [24]Therefore I tell you, all that you ask for in prayer, believe that you will receive it and it shall be yours. [25]When you stand to pray, forgive anyone against whom you have a grievance, so that your heavenly Father may in turn forgive you your transgressions." [26]

[27]They returned once more to Jerusalem. As he was walking in the temple area, the chief priests, the scribes, and the elders approached him [28]and said to him, "By what authority are you doing these things? Or who gave you this authority to do them?" [29]Jesus said to them, "I shall ask you one question. Answer me, and I will tell you by what authority I do these things. [30]Was John's baptism of heavenly or of human origin? Answer me." [31]They discussed this among themselves and said, "If we say, 'Of heavenly origin,' he will say, '[Then] why did you not believe him?' [32]But shall we say, 'Of human origin'?" —they feared the crowd, for they all thought John really was a prophet. [33]So they said to Jesus in reply, "We do not know." Then Jesus said to them, "Neither shall I tell you by what authority I do these things."

Chapter Twelve

[1]He began to speak to them in parables. "A man planted a vineyard, put a hedge around it, dug a wine press, and built a tower. Then he leased it to tenant farmers and left on a journey. [2]At the proper time he sent a servant to the tenants to obtain from them some of the produce of the vineyard. [3]But they seized him, beat him, and sent him away empty-handed. [4]Again he sent them another servant. And that one they beat over the head and treated shamefully. [5]He sent yet another whom they killed. So, too, many others; some they beat, others they killed. [6]He had one other to send, a beloved son. He sent him to them last of all, thinking, 'They will respect my son.' [7]But those tenants said to one another, 'This is the heir. Come, let us kill him, and the inheritance will be ours.' [8]So they seized him and killed

him, and threw him out of the vineyard. ⁹What [then] will the owner of the vineyard do? He will come, put the tenants to death, and give the vineyard to others. ¹⁰Have you not read this scripture passage:

'The stone that the builders rejected
has become the cornerstone;
¹¹by the Lord has this been done,
and it is wonderful in our eyes'?"

¹²They were seeking to arrest him, but they feared the crowd, for they realized that he had addressed the parable to them. So they left him and went away.

¹³They sent some Pharisees and Herodians to him to ensnare him in his speech. ¹⁴They came and said to him, "Teacher, we know that you are a truthful man and that you are not concerned with anyone's opinion. You do not regard a person's status but teach the way of God in accordance with the truth. Is it lawful to pay the census tax to Caesar or not? Should we pay or should we not pay?" ¹⁵Knowing their hypocrisy he said to them, "Why are you testing me? Bring me a denarius to look at." ¹⁶They brought one to him and he said to them, "Whose image and inscription is this?" They replied to him, "Caesar's." ¹⁷So Jesus said to them, "Repay to Caesar what belongs to Caesar and to God what belongs to God." They were utterly amazed at him.

¹⁸Some Sadducees, who say there is no resurrection, came to him and put this question to him, ¹⁹saying, "Teacher, Moses wrote for us, 'If someone's brother dies, leaving a wife but no child, his brother must take the wife and raise up descendants for his brother.' ²⁰Now there were seven brothers. The first married a woman and died, leaving no descendants. ²¹So the second married her and died, leaving no descendants, and the third likewise. ²²And the seven left no descendants. Last of all the woman also died. ²³At the resurrection [when they arise] whose wife will she be? For all seven had been married to her." ²⁴Jesus said to them, "Are you not misled because you do not know the scriptures or the power of God? ²⁵When they

rise from the dead, they neither marry nor are given in marriage, but they are like the angels in heaven. [26]As for the dead being raised, have you not read in the Book of Moses, in the passage about the bush, how God told him, 'I am the God of Abraham, [the] God of Isaac, and [the] God of Jacob'? [27]He is not God of the dead but of the living. You are greatly misled."

[28]One of the scribes, when he came forward and heard them disputing and saw how well he had answered them, asked him, "Which is the first of all the commandments?" [29]Jesus replied, "The first is this: 'Hear, O Israel! The Lord our God is Lord alone! [30]You shall love the Lord your God with all your heart, with all your soul, with all your mind, and with all your strength.' [31]The second is this: 'You shall love your neighbor as yourself.' There is no other commandment greater than these." [32]The scribe said to him, "Well said, teacher. You are right in saying, 'He is One and there is no other than he.' [33]And 'to love him with all your heart, with all your understanding, with all your strength, and to love your neighbor as yourself' is worth more than all burnt offerings and sacrifices." [34]And when Jesus saw that [he] answered with understanding, he said to him, "You are not far from the kingdom of God." And no one dared to ask him any more questions.

[35]As Jesus was teaching in the temple area he said, "How do the scribes claim that the Messiah is the son of David? [36]David himself, inspired by the holy Spirit, said:

> 'The Lord said to my lord,
> "Sit at my right hand
> until I place your enemies under your feet."'

[37]David himself calls him 'lord'; so how is he his son?" [The] great crowd heard this with delight.

[38]In the course of his teaching he said, "Beware of the scribes, who like to go around in long robes and accept greetings in the marketplaces, [39]seats of honor in synagogues, and places of honor at banquets. [40]They devour the houses of widows and, as a pretext,

recite lengthy prayers. They will receive a very severe condemnation."

[41]He sat down opposite the treasury and observed how the crowd put money into the treasury. Many rich people put in large sums. [42]A poor widow also came and put in two small coins worth a few cents. [43]Calling his disciples to himself, he said to them, "Amen, I say to you, this poor widow put in more than all the other contributors to the treasury. [44]For they have all contributed from their surplus wealth, but she, from her poverty, has contributed all she had, her whole livelihood."

Chapter Thirteen

[1]As he was making his way out of the temple area one of his disciples said to him, "Look, teacher, what stones and what buildings!" [2]Jesus said to him, "Do you see these great buildings? There will not be one stone left upon another that will not be thrown down."

[3]As he was sitting on the Mount of Olives opposite the temple area, Peter, James, John, and Andrew asked him privately, [4]"Tell us, when will this happen, and what sign will there be when all these things are about to come to an end?" [5]Jesus began to say to them, "See that no one deceives you. [6]Many will come in my name saying, 'I am he,' and they will deceive many. [7]When you hear of wars and reports of wars do not be alarmed; such things must happen, but it will not yet be the end. [8]Nation will rise against nation and kingdom against kingdom. There will be earthquakes from place to place and there will be famines. These are the beginnings of the labor pains.

[9]"Watch out for yourselves. They will hand you over to the courts. You will be beaten in synagogues. You will be arraigned before governors and kings because of me, as a witness before them. [10]But the gospel must first be preached to all nations. [11]When they lead you away and hand you over, do not worry beforehand about what you are to say. But say whatever will be given to you at that hour. For it will not be you who are speaking but the holy Spirit.

¹²Brother will hand over brother to death, and the father his child; children will rise up against parents and have them put to death. ¹³You will be hated by all because of my name. But the one who perseveres to the end will be saved.

¹⁴"When you see the desolating abomination standing where he should not (let the reader understand), then those in Judea must flee to the mountains, ¹⁵[and] a person on a housetop must not go down or enter to get anything out of his house, ¹⁶and a person in a field must not return to get his cloak. ¹⁷Woe to pregnant women and nursing mothers in those days. ¹⁸Pray that this does not happen in winter. ¹⁹For those times will have tribulation such as has not been since the beginning of God's creation until now, nor ever will be. ²⁰If the Lord had not shortened those days, no one would be saved; but for the sake of the elect whom he chose, he did shorten the days. ²¹If anyone says to you then, 'Look, here is the Messiah! Look, there he is!' do not believe it. ²²False messiahs and false prophets will arise and will perform signs and wonders in order to mislead, if that were possible, the elect. ²³Be watchful! I have told it all to you beforehand.

> ²⁴"But in those days after that tribulation
> the sun will be darkened,
> and the moon will not give its light,
> ²⁵and the stars will be falling from the sky,
> and the powers in the heavens will be shaken.

²⁶And then they will see 'the Son of Man coming in the clouds' with great power and glory, ²⁷and then he will send out the angels and gather [his] elect from the four winds, from the end of the earth to the end of the sky.

²⁸"Learn a lesson from the fig tree. When its branch becomes tender and sprouts leaves, you know that summer is near. ²⁹In the same way, when you see these things happening, know that he is near, at the gates. ³⁰Amen, I say to you, this generation will not pass away until all these things have taken place. ³¹Heaven and earth will pass away, but my words will not pass away.

³²"But of that day or hour, no one knows, neither the angels in heaven, nor the Son, but only the Father. ³³ Be watchful! Be alert! You do not know when the time will come. ³⁴It is like a man traveling abroad. He leaves home and places his servants in charge, each with his work, and orders the gatekeeper to be on the watch. ³⁵Watch, therefore; you do not know when the lord of the house is coming, whether in the evening, or at midnight, or at cockcrow, or in the morning. ³⁶May he not come suddenly and find you sleeping. ³⁷What I say to you, I say to all: 'Watch!'"

Chapter Fourteen

¹ The Passover and the Feast of Unleavened Bread were to take place in two days' time. So the chief priests and the scribes were seeking a way to arrest him by treachery and put him to death. ²They said, "Not during the festival, for fear that there may be a riot among the people."

³When he was in Bethany reclining at table in the house of Simon the leper, a woman came with an alabaster jar of perfumed oil, costly genuine spikenard. She broke the alabaster jar and poured it on his head. ⁴There were some who were indignant. "Why has there been this waste of perfumed oil? ⁵It could have been sold for more than three hundred days' wages and the money given to the poor." They were infuriated with her. ⁶Jesus said, "Let her alone. Why do you make trouble for her? She has done a good thing for me. ⁷The poor you will always have with you, and whenever you wish you can do good to them, but you will not always have me. ⁸She has done what she could. She has anticipated anointing my body for burial. ⁹Amen, I say to you, wherever the gospel is proclaimed to the whole world, what she has done will be told in memory of her."

¹⁰Then Judas Iscariot, one of the Twelve, went off to the chief priests to hand him over to them. ¹¹When they heard him they were pleased and promised to pay him money. Then he looked for an opportunity to hand him over.

[12]On the first day of the Feast of Unleavened Bread, when they sacrificed the Passover lamb, his disciples said to him, "Where do you want us to go and prepare for you to eat the Passover?" [13]He sent two of his disciples and said to them, "Go into the city and a man will meet you, carrying a jar of water. Follow him. [14]Wherever he enters, say to the master of the house, 'The Teacher says, "Where is my guest room where I may eat the Passover with my disciples?"' [15]Then he will show you a large upper room furnished and ready. Make the preparations for us there." [16]The disciples then went off, entered the city, and found it just as he had told them; and they prepared the Passover.

[17]When it was evening, he came with the Twelve. [18] And as they reclined at table and were eating, Jesus said, "Amen, I say to you, one of you will betray me, one who is eating with me." [19]They began to be distressed and to say to him, one by one, "Surely it is not I?" [20]He said to them, "One of the Twelve, the one who dips with me into the dish. [21]For the Son of Man indeed goes, as it is written of him, but woe to that man by whom the Son of Man is betrayed. It would be better for that man if he had never been born."

[22]While they were eating, he took bread, said the blessing, broke it, and gave it to them, and said, "Take it; this is my body." [23]Then he took a cup, gave thanks, and gave it to them, and they all drank from it. [24]He said to them, "This is my blood of the covenant, which will be shed for many. [25]Amen, I say to you, I shall not drink again the fruit of the vine until the day when I drink it new in the kingdom of God." [26]Then, after singing a hymn, they went out to the Mount of Olives.

[27]Then Jesus said to them, "All of you will have your faith shaken, for it is written:

'I will strike the shepherd,
and the sheep will be dispersed.'

[28]But after I have been raised up, I shall go before you to Galilee."

²⁹Peter said to him, "Even though all should have their faith shaken, mine will not be." ³⁰Then Jesus said to him, "Amen, I say to you, this very night before the cock crows twice you will deny me three times." ³¹But he vehemently replied, "Even though I should have to die with you, I will not deny you." And they all spoke similarly.

³²Then they came to a place named Gethsemane, and he said to his disciples, "Sit here while I pray." ³³He took with him Peter, James, and John, and began to be troubled and distressed. ³⁴Then he said to them, "My soul is sorrowful even to death. Remain here and keep watch." ³⁵He advanced a little and fell to the ground and prayed that if it were possible the hour might pass by him; ³⁶he said, "Abba, Father, all things are possible to you. Take this cup away from me, but not what I will but what you will." ³⁷When he returned he found them asleep. He said to Peter, "Simon, are you asleep? Could you not keep watch for one hour? ³⁸ Watch and pray that you may not undergo the test. The spirit is willing but the flesh is weak." ³⁹Withdrawing again, he prayed, saying the same thing. ⁴⁰Then he returned once more and found them asleep, for they could not keep their eyes open and did not know what to answer him. ⁴¹He returned a third time and said to them, "Are you still sleeping and taking your rest? It is enough. The hour has come. Behold, the Son of Man is to be handed over to sinners. ⁴²Get up, let us go. See, my betrayer is at hand."

⁴³Then, while he was still speaking, Judas, one of the Twelve, arrived, accompanied by a crowd with swords and clubs who had come from the chief priests, the scribes, and the elders. ⁴⁴His betrayer had arranged a signal with them, saying, "The man I shall kiss is the one; arrest him and lead him away securely." ⁴⁵He came and immediately went over to him and said, "Rabbi." And he kissed him. ⁴⁶At this they laid hands on him and arrested him. ⁴⁷One of the bystanders drew his sword, struck the high priest's servant, and cut off his ear. ⁴⁸Jesus said to them in reply, "Have you come out as against a robber, with swords and clubs, to seize me? ⁴⁹Day after day I was with you teaching in the temple area, yet you did not arrest me;

but that the scriptures may be fulfilled." ⁵⁰And they all left him and fled. ⁵¹Now a young man followed him wearing nothing but a linen cloth about his body. They seized him, ⁵²but he left the cloth behind and ran off naked.

⁵³They led Jesus away to the high priest, and all the chief priests and the elders and the scribes came together. ⁵⁴Peter followed him at a distance into the high priest's courtyard and was seated with the guards, warming himself at the fire. ⁵⁵The chief priests and the entire Sanhedrin kept trying to obtain testimony against Jesus in order to put him to death, but they found none. ⁵⁶Many gave false witness against him, but their testimony did not agree. ⁵⁷ Some took the stand and testified falsely against him, alleging, ⁵⁸"We heard him say, 'I will destroy this temple made with hands and within three days I will build another not made with hands.'" ⁵⁹Even so their testimony did not agree. ⁶⁰The high priest rose before the assembly and questioned Jesus, saying, "Have you no answer? What are these men testifying against you?" ⁶¹ But he was silent and answered nothing. Again the high priest asked him and said to him, "Are you the Messiah, the son of the Blessed One?" ⁶²Then Jesus answered,

"I am; and
'you will see the Son of Man
seated at the right hand of the Power
and coming with the clouds of heaven.'"

⁶³At that the high priest tore his garments and said, "What further need have we of witnesses? ⁶⁴You have heard the blasphemy. What do you think?" They all condemned him as deserving to die. ⁶⁵Some began to spit on him. They blindfolded him and struck him and said to him, "Prophesy!" And the guards greeted him with blows.

⁶⁶While Peter was below in the courtyard, one of the high priest's maids came along. ⁶⁷Seeing Peter warming himself, she looked intently at him and said, "You too were with the Nazarene, Jesus." ⁶⁸ But he denied it saying, "I neither know nor understand what you are talking about." So he went out into the outer court. [Then the cock

crowed.] ⁶⁹The maid saw him and began again to say to the bystanders, "This man is one of them." ⁷⁰Once again he denied it. A little later the bystanders said to Peter once more, "Surely you are one of them; for you too are a Galilean." ⁷¹He began to curse and to swear, "I do not know this man about whom you are talking." ⁷²And immediately a cock crowed a second time. Then Peter remembered the word that Jesus had said to him, "Before the cock crows twice you will deny me three times." He broke down and wept.

Chapter Fifteen

¹ As soon as morning came, the chief priests with the elders and the scribes, that is, the whole Sanhedrin, held a council. They bound Jesus, led him away, and handed him over to Pilate. ²Pilate questioned him, "Are you the king of the Jews?" He said to him in reply, "You say so." ³The chief priests accused him of many things. ⁴Again Pilate questioned him, "Have you no answer? See how many things they accuse you of." ⁵Jesus gave him no further answer, so that Pilate was amazed.

⁶Now on the occasion of the feast he used to release to them one prisoner whom they requested. ⁷A man called Barabbas was then in prison along with the rebels who had committed murder in a rebellion. ⁸The crowd came forward and began to ask him to do for them as he was accustomed. ⁹Pilate answered, "Do you want me to release to you the king of the Jews?" ¹⁰For he knew that it was out of envy that the chief priests had handed him over. ¹¹But the chief priests stirred up the crowd to have him release Barabbas for them instead. ¹²Pilate again said to them in reply, "Then what [do you want] me to do with [the man you call] the king of the Jews?" ¹³ They shouted again, "Crucify him." ¹⁴Pilate said to them, "Why? What evil has he done?" They only shouted the louder, "Crucify him." ¹⁵ So Pilate, wishing to satisfy the crowd, released Barabbas to them and, after he had Jesus scourged, handed him over to be crucified.

¹⁶The soldiers led him away inside the palace, that is, the praetorium, and assembled the whole cohort. ¹⁷They clothed him in

purple and, weaving a crown of thorns, placed it on him. ¹⁸They began to salute him with, "Hail, King of the Jews!" ¹⁹and kept striking his head with a reed and spitting upon him. They knelt before him in homage. ²⁰And when they had mocked him, they stripped him of the purple cloak, dressed him in his own clothes, and led him out to crucify him.

²¹They pressed into service a passer-by, Simon, a Cyrenian, who was coming in from the country, the father of Alexander and Rufus, to carry his cross.

²² They brought him to the place of Golgotha (which is translated Place of the Skull). ²³They gave him wine drugged with myrrh, but he did not take it. ²⁴Then they crucified him and divided his garments by casting lots for them to see what each should take. ²⁵It was nine o'clock in the morning when they crucified him. ²⁶ The inscription of the charge against him read, "The King of the Jews." ²⁷With him they crucified two revolutionaries, one on his right and one on his left. ²⁸ ²⁹ Those passing by reviled him, shaking their heads and saying, "Aha! You who would destroy the temple and rebuild it in three days, ³⁰save yourself by coming down from the cross." ³¹Likewise the chief priests, with the scribes, mocked him among themselves and said, "He saved others; he cannot save himself. ³²Let the Messiah, the King of Israel, come down now from the cross that we may see and believe." Those who were crucified with him also kept abusing him.

³³At noon darkness came over the whole land until three in the afternoon. ³⁴And at three o'clock Jesus cried out in a loud voice, *"Eloi, Eloi, lema sabachthani?"* which is translated, "My God, my God, why have you forsaken me?" ³⁵Some of the bystanders who heard it said, "Look, he is calling Elijah." ³⁶One of them ran, soaked a sponge with wine, put it on a reed, and gave it to him to drink, saying, "Wait, let us see if Elijah comes to take him down." ³⁷Jesus gave a loud cry and breathed his last. ³⁸ The veil of the sanctuary was torn in two from top to bottom. ³⁹ When the centurion who stood facing him saw how he breathed his last he said, "Truly this man was the Son of God!" ⁴⁰ There were also women looking on from a distance. Among them were Mary Magdalene, Mary the mother of the younger James and

of Joses, and Salome. [41]These women had followed him when he was in Galilee and ministered to him. There were also many other women who had come up with him to Jerusalem.

[42]When it was already evening, since it was the day of preparation, the day before the sabbath, [43]Joseph of Arimathea, a distinguished member of the council, who was himself awaiting the kingdom of God, came and courageously went to Pilate and asked for the body of Jesus. [44]Pilate was amazed that he was already dead. He summoned the centurion and asked him if Jesus had already died. [45]And when he learned of it from the centurion, he gave the body to Joseph. [46]Having bought a linen cloth, he took him down, wrapped him in the linen cloth and laid him in a tomb that had been hewn out of the rock. Then he rolled a stone against the entrance to the tomb. [47]Mary Magdalene and Mary the mother of Joses watched where he was laid.

Chapter Sixteen

[1]When the sabbath was over, Mary Magdalene, Mary, the mother of James, and Salome bought spices so that they might go and anoint him. [2]Very early when the sun had risen, on the first day of the week, they came to the tomb. [3]They were saying to one another, "Who will roll back the stone for us from the entrance to the tomb?" [4]When they looked up, they saw that the stone had been rolled back; it was very large. [5]On entering the tomb they saw a young man sitting on the right side, clothed in a white robe, and they were utterly amazed. [6]He said to them, "Do not be amazed! You seek Jesus of Nazareth, the crucified. He has been raised; he is not here. Behold the place where they laid him. [7]But go and tell his disciples and Peter, 'He is going before you to Galilee; there you will see him, as he told you.'" [8]Then they went out and fled from the tomb, seized with trembling and bewilderment. They said nothing to anyone, for they were afraid.

[9]When he had risen, early on the first day of the week, he appeared first to Mary Magdalene, out of whom he had driven seven demons. [10] She went and told his companions who were mourning

and weeping. [11]When they heard that he was alive and had been seen by her, they did not believe.

[12]After this he appeared in another form to two of them walking along on their way to the country. [13]They returned and told the others; but they did not believe them either.

[14] [But] later, as the eleven were at table, he appeared to them and rebuked them for their unbelief and hardness of heart because they had not believed those who saw him after he had been raised. [15] He said to them, "Go into the whole world and proclaim the gospel to every creature. [16]Whoever believes and is baptized will be saved; whoever does not believe will be condemned. [17]These signs will accompany those who believe: in my name they will drive out demons, they will speak new languages. [18]They will pick up serpents [with their hands], and if they drink any deadly thing, it will not harm them. They will lay hands on the sick, and they will recover."

[19]So then the Lord Jesus, after he spoke to them, was taken up into heaven and took his seat at the right hand of God. [20]But they went forth and preached everywhere, while the Lord worked with them and confirmed the word through accompanying signs.]

[And they reported all the instructions briefly to Peter's companions. Afterwards Jesus himself, through them, sent forth from east to west the sacred and imperishable proclamation of eternal salvation. Amen.]